the ORIGINAL BALTIMORE Neighborhood COOKBOOK

by

Irina Smith & Ann Hazan

Designed & Illustrated by Amy Blake

CAMINO BOOKS
Philadelphia

Manufactured in the United States of America

3 4 5 94 93

Library of Congress Cataloging-in-Publication Data

Smith, Irina, 1942
The original Baltimore neighborhood cookbook / Irina Smith & Ann Hazan.
p. cm.
Includes index.
1. Cookery, American. 2. Cookery—Maryland—Baltimore.
I. Hazan, Ann, 1946- II. Title.
TX715.S6528

641.5973—dc20 91-8913

ISBN 0-940159-13-9 (paper)

This book is available at a special discount on bulk purchases for promotional, business and educational use. For information, write to:

Publisher
Camino Books, Inc.
P.O. Box 59026
Philadelphia, PA 19102

Cover recipes: Shrimp with Linguine, p. 179.
Steamed Blue Crabs, p. 113.
Southern Strawberry Tart, p. 228.

Cover photo: Dennis Degnan

To Baltimore and her people
Lords and Ladies all!

Contents

Introduction

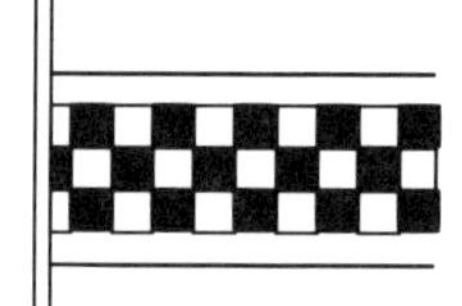

What better way to acquaint oneself with Baltimore than to walk through its distinctive neighborhoods, rich in ethnic heritage, many homes of which are graced with beautiful white marble steps, and talk to Baltimoreans about. . . what else?. . . food! What strikes one almost immediately is that Baltimore is a mixture of graceful Southern traditions and Northern economic progressiveness. Baltimore's famous poet Ogden Nash put it this way: "The top of the South and the toe of the North, it constantly teeters back and forth."

Baltimore has always had its historical and scenic sights, and many of the neighborhoods have undergone exciting changes, such as the development of the magnificent harbor. But, even with these changes, Baltimore remains a city of ethnic neighborhoods, with a local cuisine all its own, famous for Chesapeake Bay seafood dishes and boasting some of the best crab cakes in the country. One of our many memorable experiences was to sit down in a local crab house and order a dozen steamed blue crabs that arrived at our newspaper-covered table in a tantalizing aroma of mixed spices. We proceeded to pick our way through the crabs and with wooden hammers crack the claws to remove the delicious, delectable meat from them. This was washed down with an ice-cold pitcher of local beer.

In 1632, Charles I granted the territory around the Chesapeake Bay to George Calvert, who had been knighted in 1617 and who later became Lord Baltimore. The city of Baltimore is named after him and was founded in 1729.

The small town grew quickly. By the mid-1800s the Port of Baltimore was bustling with world trade and had become an active point of disembarkation for immigrants from many lands and continents. Another factor adding to Baltimore's rapid growth was railroading. The famous B & O (Baltimore and Ohio), America's first railroad, began in Baltimore.

As with most large port and railroad cities, the large influx of immigrants resettled in a city of many ethnic groups and nationalities grouped into neighborhoods, which in Baltimore number in the hundreds. A few listed in the historical records include Butcher's Hill, Govans, Fells Point, Little Italy, Lauraville, Ridgely's Delight, Pigtown, Little Lithuania, Harlem Park, Dickeyville, and Otterbein. As is evidenced in our cookbook, we found a wonderful diversity in the cuisines of Baltimore, from hyphenated Americans everywhere—Polish, German, Jewish, Italian, Greek, Indian, African, Korean, and Chinese, to name just a few—who have contributed to the city's store of good foods.

Baltimore, known for its markets, is the home of the famous Lexington Market and others including Hollins, Cross Street, Belair, Broadway, and Lafayette. Each has its own unique personality and devoted patrons who shop faithfully even if they have moved from the area. We discovered that these markets are very diversified and carry many of the interesting ethnic ingredients that we needed in order to test all the wonderful recipes included in this book.

Through *The Original Baltimore Neighborhood Cookbook* we hope to keep alive the spirit of treasured family recipes and ethnic cuisine. Now it's your turn to experience some of Baltimore's traditional and ethnic neighborhood foods. Happy cooking!

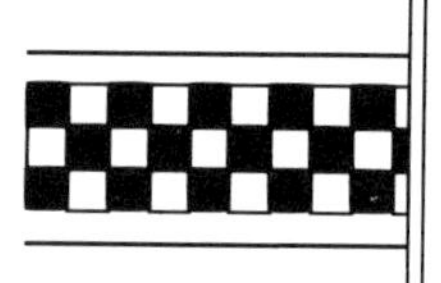

Acknowledgments

To collect the recipes for this book, we traveled miles by car and foot through Baltimore's neighborhoods tasting and testing the favorite recipes from the people who live and work there. We visited private homes, local shops, places of worship, medical centers, neighborhood restaurants, diners, and taverns to bring you appetizers, entrees, desserts and a variety of ethnic dishes for every season and occasion. We watched the preparation of each recipe and then tested, measured ingredients, and standardized these family favorites for all of us to follow in our own kitchens and enjoy in our homes.

We would like to thank all the wonderful people in the many Baltimore neighborhoods we visited, who willingly and generously shared with us, and now with you, their most treasured recipes. We hope no one has been omitted inadvertently.

Fernando Alves do Rio *Highlandtown*
Mae Anderson *Freedom Way/N.E. Baltimore*
Antoinette Athos *Locust Point*
Abraham Azab *Bolton*
Karen Brown *Canton*
Ed Byer *Hollins Market*
Lisa Kargulian *Collidge Roland Park*
Louise Chen *Waverly*
Joan Cornish *Little Flower*
Paul Devine *Lexington Market*
Esther Dilegge *Belaire Market*
Ester Duke Tabacco *Edmondson Village*
Gloria Dutton *Pimlico*
Ali Ehteshami *Highlandtown*
John Fetcher *Chales Center*
Agnes Fleming *N.W. Baltimore*
Edith Friedman *Walbrook*
Sis Ganjon *Cross Street Market*
Sally Gibson *Union Square*
Mike Girolamo *Little Italy*
Bill Green *Cross Street Market*
Benjamin Groff *Lexington Market*
Peggy Hargrove *Mt Washington/Cheswolde*
Carol Hoared *South Baltimore*
Kate Hodge *Mount Vernon*
Michael Jermann *Hollins Market*
Juh Yoon *Waverly*
Averil Kadis *Fells Point*
Mel Kalinski *Canton*
Keun Kang Yoon *Upton*
Robert & Mary Kinsey *Hollins Park*
Barbara Lang *Highlandtown*

ACKNOWLEDGMENTS

Amy Lee *Waverly*
Ling Wang *Waverly*
Glenora Mckenzie *Govans*
Helen McNeal *Little Flower*
Barbara Miegon *Howard Park*
George Moser *Hollins Market*
Eric Oosterwijk *Hollins Market*
Earl Oppel *Corn Beef Row*
Marge Orem *Edmondson Village*
Sophie Para *Broad Street Market*
Min Plakoporis *Waverly*
The Enoch Pratt *Free Library*
Alice Pyle *Mt. Vernon*
Mary Pyle *Mt. Vernon*
Mohamid Rangbar *Highlandtown*
Virginia Retzer *Roland Park*
Linda Rogers *Upton*
Colleen Rosenbach *Locust Point*
Steven Ross *Charles Center*
Angie Rounis *Highlandtown*
Ashok Sahni *Charles Center*
Dee Sfakianos *Fells Point*
Barbara Singer *South Baltimore*
Red Soistman *Morrell Park*
Reoko Takahashi *Charles Center*
Ted Talbert *Roland Park*
Sophia Tsamouras *Hollins Market*
Nick Vaccaro *Little Italy*
Eva Vatakis *Highlandtown*
Frank Vellegia *Little Italy*
Alberta Williams *Irvington*
Ying Xu *Charles Village*
Julia Zenick *South Baltimore*

Appetizers

Fells Point

Fells Point is a waterfront area located near the Inner Harbor. It is a quaint neighborhood with cobblestone streets, which was founded as a separate town in 1763 by the Fell family. Many of the houses and shops are being restored, and Fells Point has been the home of the Broadway Food Market for many years. Immigrants including Italians, Poles, Jews, and Greeks settled here.

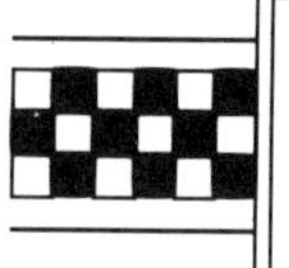

Crab Nibble Dip

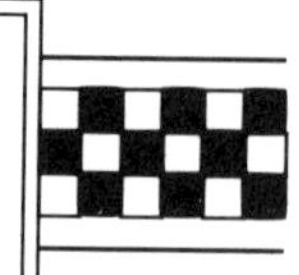

From Morrell Park **_Makes about 4 cups_**

A delicious dip which should be made ahead so that the flavors blend.

1/2 pound (2 sticks) unsalted butter
1/2 pound shredded cheddar cheese
2 tablespoons mayonnaise
1/2 teaspoon Worcestershire sauce
1 teaspoon Old Bay seasoning
1/2 teaspoon garlic powder
1 pound lump crabmeat, picked through for cartilage

1. Cream butter until smooth. Add remaining ingredients except for crabmeat and mix thoroughly.
2. Fold in crabmeat and toss gently. Serve.

Serving suggestion: Serve with fresh vegetables, crackers or pita bread.

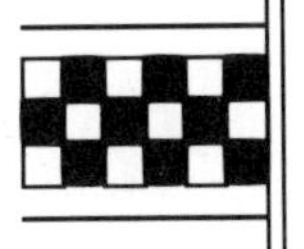

Clam Bake

From Morrell Park ***Makes 36***

Hungarian paprika has a less bitter taste than many other varieties of paprikas and gives a more subtle taste to many dishes.

3 dozen littleneck clams, scrubbed clean
2 cups Italian flavored breadcrumbs
1 teaspoon Hungarian paprika
1/4 teaspoon red pepper flakes
2 tablespoons olive oil
2 large garlic cloves, minced
1/2 pound bacon, finely diced

1. Preheat oven to 350°.
2. Steam clams until shells open. Remove clams from shells. Separate shells, place clams on one half of the shell, and discard the other half.
3. In a bowl, combine breadcrumbs, paprika, red pepper, olive oil and garlic.
4. Arrange clam shells on a baking sheet, spread some of the mixture on each clam, and sprinkle with diced bacon. Bake for approximately 20 minutes. Serve at once.

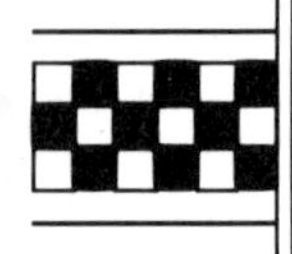

Stuffed Mushrooms

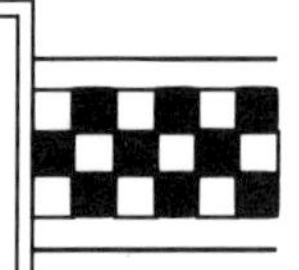

From Cross Street Market, Federal Hill **Chinese** ***Makes 24***

Water chestnuts are the bulbs of wild rushes. Fresh water chestnuts are quite different from canned in that they are sweeter in taste and have a more crisp texture. Fresh water chestnuts are available in most Oriental grocery stores; if you come across them do try in dishes that call for water chestnuts.

24 large mushrooms, wiped clean, stems removed
4 tablespoons unsalted butter, melted
3/4–1 pound ground lamb
2 tablespoons minced green onions (use green part also)
1/4 cup minced water chestnuts
1/8 teaspoon white pepper
1/4 teaspoon ground ginger
2 teaspoons soy sauce
1/4 cup chicken broth
Sesame seeds for sprinkling

1. Preheat oven to 375°.
2. Brush mushroom caps with butter and place in a shallow baking pan.
3. In a bowl, combine lamb, green onions, water chestnuts, pepper, ginger, soy sauce and chicken broth and mix well.
4. Stuff mushroom caps and sprinkle with sesame seeds. Bake for approximately 25 minutes or until lightly browned and lamb is cooked through. Serve.

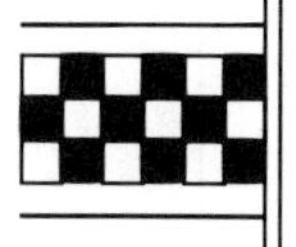

Honeyed Chicken Wings

From Morrell Park ***Serves 4–6***

These tasty chicken wings can be prepared ahead of time and served at room temperature or heated through.

10–12 chicken wings, tip end removed
1/4 cup orange juice
1/4 cup soy sauce
1/4 cup honey
4 scallions, cut into 2-inch pieces
3 garlic cloves, crushed
1/2 teaspoon chopped ginger

1. Divide chicken wings into 2 pieces.
2. In a large skillet, brown chicken pieces and pour off any fat. Add remaining ingredients, cover and simmer for about 10 minutes. Remove lid and continue cooking another 20–25 minutes or until liquid has evaporated and chicken is cooked through. Serve.

Marinated Duck Breast

From Union Square **Serves 4–6**

Instead of making chutney, though preferable, try using your favorite store-bought chutney with this dish. Also, instead of curry mayonnaise, a good currant jelly heated with a little butter and some red wine may be served. Chicken breasts may be substituted for duck.

SAUCE
1 cup mayonnaise
1 tablespoon curry powder or to taste
1 tablespoon chutney (page 192)

2 whole duck breasts, boned and skinned
1/4 cup teriyaki
3–4 slices fresh ginger
2 tablespoons red wine vinegar
3/4 cup olive oil
2 tablespoons unsalted butter for frying

1. To make sauce, combine all ingredients, mix well and refrigerate.
2. Place duck breasts in a glass bowl. Pour remaining ingredients over duck and marinate 6–8 hours or overnight in refrigerator.
3. Remove from refrigerator 2 hours before cooking. Lift duck from marinade and cut into thin strips.
4. In a skillet, melt butter, add duck strips a few at a time and quickly stir-fry about 1–2 minutes. Do not overcook or duck will toughen and dry out. Serve on toothpicks with sauce.

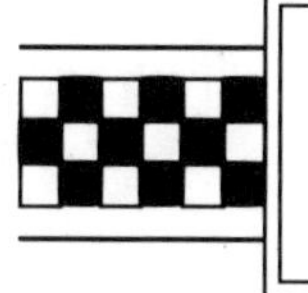

Spring Rolls

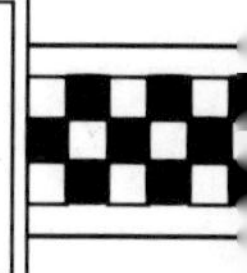

From Charles Village **Chinese** ***Makes 20 rolls***

Chinese vinegars are usually fermented from rice. Black vinegar has a stronger taste and color with a slight sweetness compared to other vinegars and is mostly used in dipping sauces.

DIPPING SAUCE
4 tablespoons black vinegar*
1 teaspoon soy sauce*
2 teaspoons sugar
2 tablespoons chicken stock
1 teaspoon sesame oil*

1 pound thinly sliced pork
2 tablespoons peanut oil
3 cups shredded Chinese cabbage
1 8-ounce can bamboo shoots,* shredded
6 mushrooms, thinly sliced
Salt to taste
1 tablespoon cornstarch mixed with 1 1/2 tablespoons water
20 egg roll wrappers*
Peanut oil for frying

1. Prepare dipping sauce. In a bowl, combine all ingredients until well blended. Set aside.
2. In a skillet, add 1 tablespoon of the peanut oil and stir-fry pork for about 2–3 minutes. Remove from pan and reserve.
3. Add remaining tablespoon of oil, stir-fry cabbage, bamboo shoots and mushrooms, sprinkle with salt and 2 tablespoons of water and continue cooking for 1–2 minutes. Add reserved pork and cornstarch mixture to skillet and stir-fry another 1–2 minutes or until slightly thickened. Mixture should be moist; if necessary, add a little more water. Cool.
4. Peel off one egg roll wrapper and place on work surface with a point facing you. The square wrapper now

looks like a triangle. Place 1 tablespoon of mixture in the center and fold end over filling, then fold sides in and roll firmly. Slightly dampen edges to seal tightly. Repeat with remaining wrappers.

5. Heat oil, approximately 2 inches deep, in a wok or skillet. Fry rolls a few at a time until lightly browned, about 1–2 minutes on each side.
6. Serve with dipping sauce.

*Available at Oriental food stores.

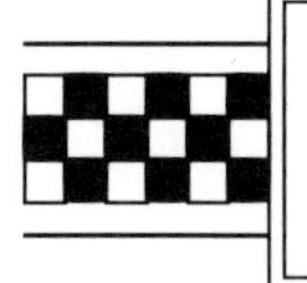

Chopped Chicken Liver

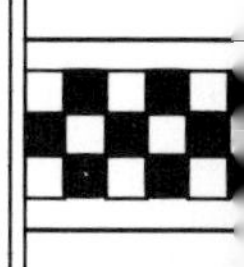

From Corned Beef Row **Jewish** ***Makes 3 cups***

To render chicken fat, place chicken skins or about 6–8 chicken wings in a skillet and cook over low heat very slowly until fat renders out.

1 pound chicken livers
Kosher salt
1 medium onion, chopped
2 hard-cooked eggs
1 teaspoon salt
1/8 teaspoon freshly ground pepper
1 tablespoon rendered chicken fat

1. Cut away fatty tissue from livers and rinse. Sprinkle with Kosher salt.
2. Bring a saucepan of water to a boil, add chicken livers and poach for about 5 minutes or until cooked. Drain.
3. In a food processor, add chopped onion, chicken livers, cooked eggs, salt and pepper. Blend until smooth. Add chicken fat and blend again until very smooth. Serve.

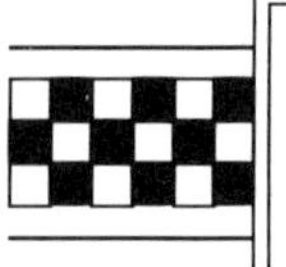

Onion Tomato Tart

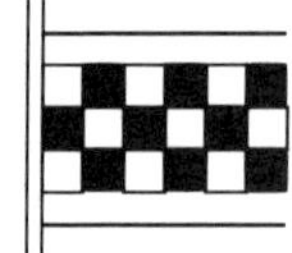

From Union Square ***Serves 6–8***

This delectable onion tart makes an excellent do-ahead appetizer. It can also be served as a first course or for a light lunch. Because of the long slow cooking, the onions caramelize and take on a delicate sweetness.

PASTRY SHELL
1 1/4 cups all-purpose flour
Pinch of cinnamon (optional)
Pinch of salt
6 tablespoons cold unsalted butter, cut into pieces
2 tablespoons cold vegetable shortening
3–4 tablespoons ice water

FILLING
1/4 cup olive oil
5–7 onions, thinly sliced
2 garlic cloves, minced
1 28-ounce can Italian plum tomatoes, drained, with seeds removed
1 tablespoon tomato paste
1/2 teaspoon sugar
Pinch of dried herbs (oregano, thyme or basil)
Freshly ground pepper to taste
Breadcrumbs
1–2 tablespoons Parmesan cheese
1 2-ounce can anchovy fillets, drained (optional)
6–8 black olives, pitted and sliced in half

1. To make shell, combine flour, cinnamon (if used) and salt in a bowl. Cut in butter and shortening until mixture resembles coarse meal. Sprinkle ice water over flour, one tablespoon at a time, tossing with a fork until it comes together to form a dough. Gather dough into a ball, cover with plastic wrap, flatten slightly and chill 10 minutes. On a floured surface, roll dough to fit into a 9-inch tart pan with a removable bottom. Crimp excess dough from top of fluted edges. Prick bottom of dough with a fork, cover and chill 30 minutes before baking.

2. Meanwhile prepare filling. In a skillet, heat the oil over medium heat until hot. Add onions and garlic, cook stirring for 2 minutes, reduce heat to low, cover skillet and cook for 45 minutes, stirring occasionally.

3. In a small saucepan, cook tomatoes with tomato paste, sugar and herbs about 20 minutes until reduced.

4. Combine tomatoes with cooked onions. Season with freshly ground pepper.

5. Preheat oven to 425°.

6. Remove shell from refrigerator. Sprinkle with breadcrumbs and spread onion mixture evenly in shell. Sprinkle with cheese and place olives and anchovies (if desired) decoratively on top.

7. Bake for approximately 30–40 minutes or until crust is golden brown. Remove from oven. Cool slightly, cut into wedges and serve.

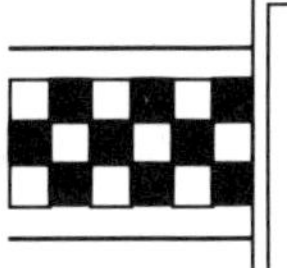

Classic Swiss Fondue

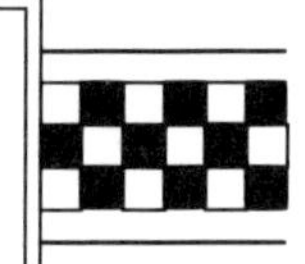

From Cross Street Market, Federal Hill ***Serves 4–6***

"La Religieuse" is the crust which forms at the bottom of the finished fondue. To many fondue eaters this is a delicacy that should be shared equally between everyone. One popular Swiss tradition is if a woman loses her bread in the fondue, she must kiss the man to her right and the man so doing must kiss the woman to his right, and so on. . . .

- 1 garlic clove, halved
- 1 1/2 cups dry white wine
- 1 tablespoon lemon juice
- 1/2 pound grated Swiss Gruyere
- 1/4 pound grated Emmenthaler
- 1/4 pound grated Appenzeller or Cantal
- 3 tablespoons flour
- 3 tablespoons kirsch
- Salt and pepper to taste
- Freshly grated nutmeg to taste
- 1 loaf French bread, cut into 1-inch cubes

1. Rub inside of a fondue pot or chafing dish with cut side of garlic. Pour in wine and lemon juice and heat gently over low heat. Do not bring to boil.
2. In a plastic bag or bowl, combine cheeses with flour and shake or toss to mix thoroughly. Gradually add to wine, stirring continuously until cheese melts. Add kirsch, salt, pepper and nutmeg to taste.
3. Keep fondue warm over low heat. Serve with bread cubes. If mixture gets too thick, add some additional warm wine and stir until smooth.

Hommus (Chick-Pea Spread)

From Washington Hill **Lebanese** ***Makes 3 cups***

An interesting variation to this traditional Lebanese favorite is the addition of tamari sauce and Old Bay seasoning. For a thinner consistency add enough olive oil for easy spreading.

15-ounce can chick-peas with juice
2 garlic cloves, crushed
8 tablespoons tahini*
2 tablespoons fresh lemon juice
2 teaspoons tamari soy sauce*
1/4 teaspoon salt
Pinch of cayenne pepper
Pinch of Old Bay seasoning
2 scallions, chopped

1. Place all ingredients except scallions in a food processor and mix until well blended.
2. Add chopped scallions and whiz briefly. Serve.

Serving suggestion: Serve with pita bread or assorted fresh vegetables.

*Available at specialty food stores.

Baba Ghanoush (Eggplant Dip)

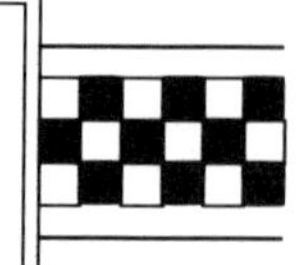

From Bolton **Middle Eastern** ***Makes 2 cups***

Eggplants can be bitter but also contain a lot of moisture. Salting eliminates both problems. Dice or slice eggplants depending on recipe, place in a colander, sprinkle with salt and allow to drain for about 1 hour. Rinse, pat dry and use as directed.

2 medium eggplants
3 garlic cloves, crushed
1/2 teaspoon cumin
1/2 teaspoon coriander
1/4 cup fresh lime or lemon juice
1/3 cup tahini*
About 1/4 cup olive oil

1. Set oven to broil. Place eggplants on an aluminum foil-lined cookie sheet and broil until skins are charred and eggplants are soft, approximately 1/2 hour (eggplants should be turned several times during cooking). Another method for cooking eggplants is to brush them with oil and wrap in aluminum foil. Place on a baking sheet and bake at 350° until soft, approximately 1/2 hour.
2. Cool eggplants and peel. Squeeze gently to remove seeds and bitter juices.
3. In a food processor or blender, combine eggplant, garlic, cumin, coriander, lime juice and tahini. Purée, adding olive oil in a slow, steady stream to form a smooth and creamy consistency.
4. Adjust seasonings to taste and serve.

Serving suggestions: Serve with pita wedges or assorted vegetables.

*Available at Middle Eastern and specialty food stores.

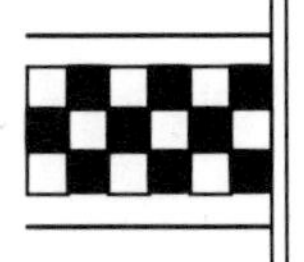

Felafel

From Bolton **Lebanese** ***Serves 4***

Sesame paste is a thick paste made from sesame seeds that have been pulverized. Cumin has a pungent, spicy-sweet aroma and a brownish-green color. It is a key ingredient in many Middle Eastern foods.

TAHINI SAUCE
1 cup sesame paste
Juice of 1 lime
2 cloves garlic, minced
1/8 teaspoon cumin
1/8 teaspoon coriander
Water
Corn oil

1 cup green split peas, soaked in water for 24–48 hours and drained
2 cloves garlic, minced
1/2 cup chopped parsley
3 scallions, chopped
1/3 cup chopped leeks
1 teaspoon cumin
1 teaspoon salt
1/2–1 teaspoon ground coriander
1/2 teaspoon baking soda
1 egg
Vegetable oil for frying

1. Prepare tahini sauce. In a blender or food processor, combine all ingredients except oil and water and whiz until mixed. Add about 2 tablespoons water and slowly pour in enough oil until mixture is the consistency of mayonnaise. Reserve.
2. In a food processor or blender, purée split peas until smooth.
3. Place purée in a mixing bowl and add remaining ingredients. Mix thoroughly.
4. Form mixture into balls about 1-inch in diameter.

5. In a skillet, heat oil approximately 2 inches deep and add felafel balls a few at a time. Cook until golden in color, turning them once or twice. Drain on paper towels.
6. Serve with tahini sauce.

Baltimore City Markets

Market houses date from the early 1800s when the first settlers wanted to establish places of barter and sale. Since then the markets have grown and undergone many changes. Where once the markets housed only stalls selling fruits, vegetables, fish and meats, they now also offer a selection of prepared foods and baked goods, cheeses from all over the world and game, in addition to featuring a tantalizing mosaic of local and ethnic delicacies such as deep-fried stuffed hardshell crabs, Maryland fried chicken, Polish pierogies, and Greek baklava. The famous Lexington Market, founded in 1782, is one of the oldest continuously operating markets in the United States. Other Baltimore markets include The Broadway, Cross Street, Hollins, Belair, and Lafayette. Many of the stalls have been operated by successive generations of the same family for more than a century. The markets are frequented by neighborhood shoppers as well as by visitors to the city.

Soups and Stocks

Federal Hill

Federal Hill is located close to the harbor area. In 1788 about 4000 Marylanders celebrated the ratification of the Federal constitution there, hence the name Federal Hill. Many historic monuments and statues can be found in this area.

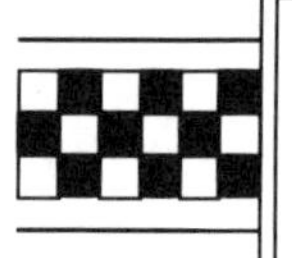

Baltimore Borscht

From Roland Park ***Serves 6–8***

This recipe is of mixed ethnicity, combining several different ingredients from various traditional borscht recipes.

3 cups water
4 cups beef broth
1 small cabbage, shredded
2 large onions, diced
4 16-ounce cans beets, finely diced
1 46-ounce can V-8 juice
2 tablespoons red wine vinegar
3 bay leaves, crushed
Dash of sherry
1 cup sour cream

1. In a stockpot, combine water, beef broth, cabbage and onions. Boil for 5–10 minutes. Add beets, reduce heat to simmer, add remaining ingredients except for sour cream and cook until vegetables are tender, about 1 hour.
2. Remove from heat and let stand 1 hour. To serve hot, reheat and stir in sour cream. To serve cold, chill and serve with a dollop of sour cream.

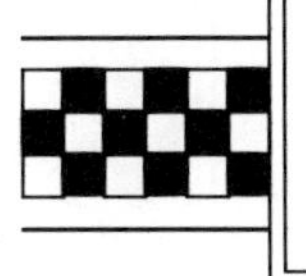

Gazpacho

From Canton **Spanish** ***Serves 6–8***

This soup can be made by chopping all of the vegetables very finely by hand and combining with the remaining ingredients. Make croutons by cubing Italian or French bread and frying in a garlic-flavored olive oil. Instead of croutons, finely minced vegetables can be used as a garnish.

- 4 Italian plum tomatoes, peeled, seeded and sliced in half
- 1 small green bell pepper, seeded and coarsely chopped (or 1/2 green and 1/2 red pepper)
- 1 small onion, quartered
- 1 small cucumber, peeled, seeded and coarsely chopped
- 2 celery stalks, coarsely chopped
- 1 tablespoon fresh parsley
- 1 teaspoon chopped chives
- 1 garlic clove
- 1/4 teaspoon tarragon
- 2 tablespoons olive oil
- 2 tablespoons red wine vinegar
- 1/2 teaspoon salt
- Freshly ground pepper to taste
- 2 dashes Tabasco or to taste
- 1 1/2 cups tomato juice
- 1/2 cup V-8 juice
- Croutons (garnish)

1. In the bowl of a food processor fitted with a metal blade, place all ingredients. Process until the vegetables are very finely chopped but not to the purée stage.
2. Pour soup into a bowl, cover and refrigerate at least 4 hours.
3. Serve in chilled cups or bowls and top with croutons.

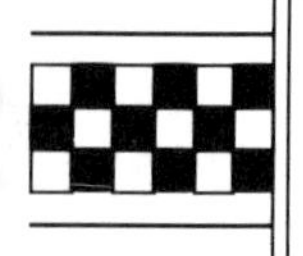

15-Bean Soup

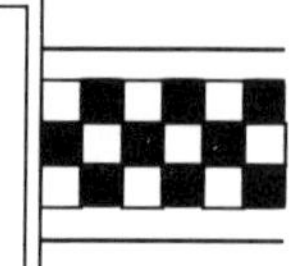

From Pimlico **Serves 6–8**

Gourmet beans can be purchased in a package and are a combination of dried beans including great northern, marrow, lima, kidney, split peas and black-eyed peas.

1 pound gourmet beans
1 ham hock, split
Water
1 onion, chopped
2 celery stalks, sliced
2 carrots, sliced
Salt and pepper to taste
2 tablespoons soy sauce

1. Place beans in a large bowl and cover with water. Allow to soak overnight.
2. In a large stockpot, place ham hock and add 1 1/2 quarts of water to cover. Bring to a boil, reduce heat and simmer 1 hour.
3. Add onions, celery and carrots to pot. Drain beans and add to pot. Season with salt and pepper (little salt may be needed because of the ham hocks). Simmer until beans are tender, approximately 2 hours. If needed, add more hot water during cooking.
4. Add soy sauce to bean soup, adjust seasoning and serve.

Serving suggestion: Serve with Baltimore cheese bread (page 203).

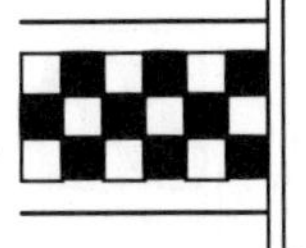

Lemon Lentil Soup

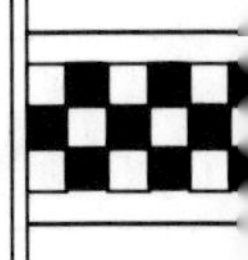

From Roland Park ***Serves 6–8***

Lentils and beans in general are nutritious and full of protein. In this recipe the addition of thinly sliced lemons adds a refreshing flavor.

4 quarts water
10 beef bouillon cubes
2 2/3 cups dry lentils, picked through carefully for stones and then rinsed thoroughly before using
2 large lemons, thinly sliced, seeds removed
2 medium onions, thinly sliced
1 pound mushrooms, thinly sliced
2 tablespoons chopped fresh parsley
1 tablespoon oregano
5 bay leaves, crushed
1 cup white wine
1 tablespoon olive oil
Salt and pepper to taste

1. In a stockpot, combine the water, bouillon cubes and lentils. Bring to a boil, reduce heat and cook lentils for 20 minutes.
2. Add lemons, onions, mushrooms, parsley, oregano and bay leaves and cook another 20–25 minutes or until vegetables and lentils are tender.
3. Drizzle with olive oil and add salt and pepper. Simmer an additional 5 minutes. Serve.

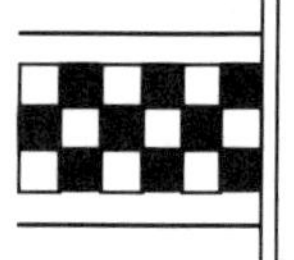

Hearty Lentil Soup

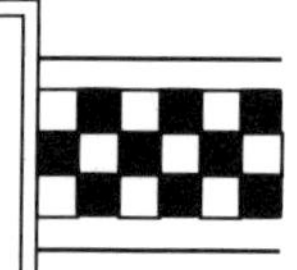

From Mt. Washington **Serves 4–6**

Japanese soy sauce is made only from soy beans, wheat and salt, and is then fermented and aged. It adds a delicious flavor to this lentil soup.

- 2 carrots, diced
- 1 large onion, diced
- 1 small sweet potato, diced
- 1 cup chopped fresh parsley
- 2 cups lentils
- 2 1/2 quarts water
- 1/4 cup sliced mushrooms
- 2 teaspoons garlic powder
- 1/2 teaspoon tarragon
- 1/2 teaspoon oregano
- 1/2 teaspoon basil
- 1/2 cup tamari* (Japanese soy sauce)

1. In a large saucepan, layer the carrots, onions, sweet potatoes and parsley.
2. Rinse the lentils and add to the pot. Pour in water and bring to a boil. Lower heat and simmer for 40 minutes or until lentils are almost cooked.
3. Add mushrooms, garlic powder, tarragon, oregano and basil. Simmer for another 15–20 minutes. When lentils are cooked, add tamari, stir and serve.

*Available at Oriental and specialty food stores.

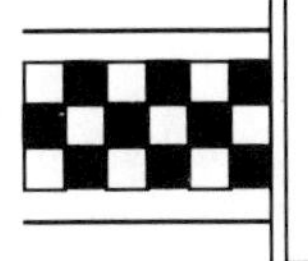

Avgolemono Soup (Egg/Lemon Soup)

From Highlandtown **Greek** ***Serves 6–8***

Avgolemono is a traditional Greek soup. Avgo *is the Greek word for egg and* lemone *for lemon. To reheat this soup, the secret is to simmer gently. Boiling will cause the egg to curdle.*

1 3 1/2-pound chicken, rinsed inside and out
6 cups water
2 celery stalks, sliced
1/3 cup uncooked rice
Salt and pepper to taste
3 eggs, separated
Juice of 2 lemons

1. Place chicken in a stockpot and add water. Bring to a boil, reduce heat and simmer gently, skimming residue as necessary. Cook approximately 1 hour or until chicken is tender.
2. Remove chicken and use for another recipe or serve as is.
3. To the broth, add the celery, rice, salt and pepper to taste and boil over medium heat until rice is cooked, about 20 minutes.
4. Beat the egg whites until stiff peaks form. Add egg yolks and mix thoroughly. Slowly add lemon juice to eggs and mix.
5. Pour in approximately 2 cups of the chicken broth, a ladle at a time, to the egg/lemon mixture, beating constantly until the mixture warms slightly. Then pour the warmed egg/lemon mixture back into the hot broth. (This technique will neutralize the egg/lemon mixture and prevent it from curdling.) Heat gently. Do not boil.
6. Adjust seasoning and serve.

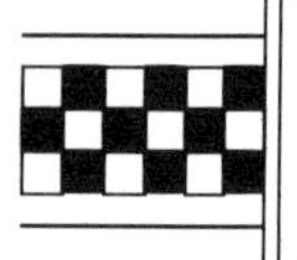

Zupa Szczawiowa (Sorrel Soup)

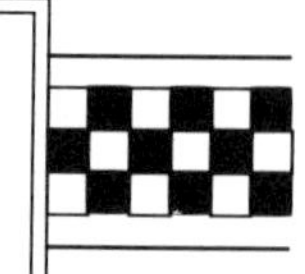

From Fells Point **Polish** ***Serves 4***

Sorrel has a slightly bitter and lemony taste. The younger, tender leaves are good for using in a salad.

4 tablespoons butter
1 pound sorrel, rinsed, chopped and stems removed
1 small potato, peeled and quartered
6 cups beef stock
Salt and pepper
4 egg yolks
4 cups sour cream or yogurt

1. In a large saucepan, melt butter and add sorrel. Cover and cook until wilted, about 5 minutes. In a food processor or blender, purée sorrel. Return to saucepan.
2. Boil potato until cooked. Drain and mash thoroughly. Add to sorrel purée and mix. Pour in stock, season with salt and pepper and simmer for 10 minutes, whisking occasionaly to prevent lumps from forming.
3. In a bowl, beat egg yolks. Add a little of the soup broth to the yolks and whisk with a fork. Then pour the egg mixture slowly into the simmering soup. (For a thinner consistency, add more stock to soup.)
4. Add sour cream or yogurt to the broth and stir. Serve.

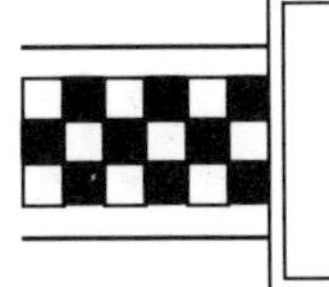

Minestrone

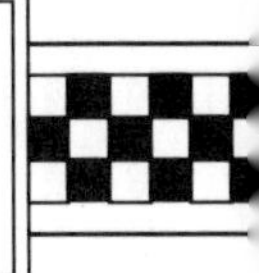

From Highlandtown **Italian** ***Serves 6–8***

This soup freezes well. An equal proportion of fresh vegetables may be used instead of the frozen mixed vegetables. This is a very hearty soup and a meal in itself.

1 medium onion, coarsely chopped
3 celery stalks, chopped
2 carrots, cut into 1/2-inch-thick rounds
2 tablespoons olive oil
1 16-ounce package frozen mixed vegetables
1/4 head small cabbage, sliced
1 19-ounce can chick-peas, undrained
1 19-ounce can red kidney beans, undrained
1 19-ounce can white kidney beans, undrained
1 11-ounce can zesty tomato soup
1 packet beef onion soup mix
1 cup water
Black pepper to taste
1 cup macaroni (elbow, ditalini or orzo)
Freshly grated Parmesan cheese to taste

1. In a stockpot over low heat, gently sauté onion, celery and carrots in olive oil for 10–15 minutes. Stir in frozen mixed vegetables and cabbage. Simmer 5 minutes. Add peas and beans, tomato soup, onion soup mix and water. Bring to a boil, reduce heat and simmer 1 hour. Season with black pepper.
2. Add macaroni and cook about 15–20 minutes or until pasta is tender. Add more water (1 cup or more as needed) to reach desired consistency.
3. Sprinkle with grated cheese and serve.

Serving suggestion: Serve with Baltimore cheese bread (page 203).

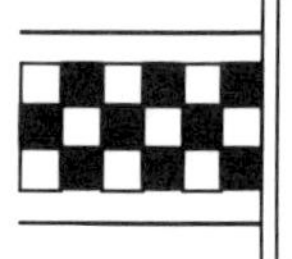

Oyster Soup

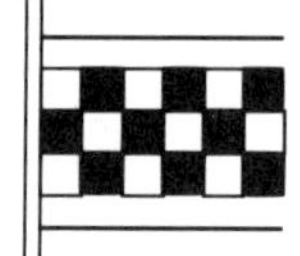

From Lexington Market ***Serves 4***

There are many varieties of oysters to be found. One of the varieties is the famous chincoteagues. Always buy oysters with shells tightly closed. Fresh shucked oysters may be eaten raw, but if frozen they should only be used for soups and stews.

1 quart shucked oysters with juice
2 tablespoons butter
2 cups half-and-half
2 cups milk
1 teaspoon celery salt
1 teaspoon chopped fresh parsley

1. In a skillet, sauté oysters with juice in butter until the edges of oysters are slightly curled, about 1–2 minutes. Remove from heat.
2. In a saucepan, pour in half-and-half and milk and simmer until just heated through. Add celery salt, parsley and oysters and simmer over low heat for about 5 minutes. Do not boil.
3. Serve.

Serving suggestion: Very good with beaten biscuits (page 202).

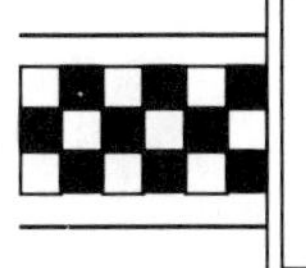

Whiskey Hill Crab Chowder

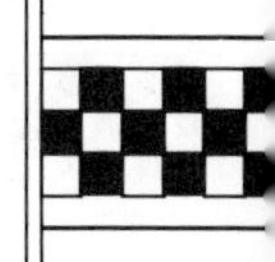

From Canton ***Serves 6–8***

This is a light and refreshing chowder which freezes beautifully. An easy way of removing the kernels from the corn is by using a sharp paring knife. If fresh corn is unavailable, canned corn may be substituted.

1 medium onion, chopped
4 tablespoons butter
6 ripe medium-sized tomatoes, peeled and coarsely chopped
5 cups chicken broth, preferably homemade (page 32)
3 sprigs fresh or 1 teaspoon dried thyme
Kernels from 3 ears of white corn
1 pound lump crabmeat, picked through for cartilage
Dash of Tabasco
Salt and pepper to taste
Fresh chopped parsley or chervil to taste

1. In a large saucepan, saute the onion in butter until transparent.
2. Add tomatoes, cover pan and simmer for approximately 5 minutes.
3. Add chicken broth and thyme and bring to a boil. Stir in corn, crabmeat and Tabasco, cover and simmer gently for 5 minutes. Add salt and pepper to taste. Simmer uncovered for an additional 5–10 minutes.
4. Sprinkle with chopped parsley or chervil and serve immediately.

Serving suggestion: Serve with Italian bread (page 200).

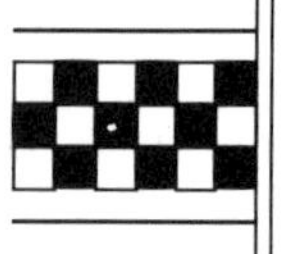

Clam Chowder

From Mount Vernon ***Serves 6***

This soup has a slightly piquant taste due to the saffron and pepper flakes. Pancetta, an Italian cured bacon, adds to the flavor of this delicious chowder.

1/4 pound pancetta,* finely diced
4 garlic cloves, minced
1/2 cup chopped scallions
1/2 cup chopped leeks
1/2 cup chopped green peppers
1/2 cup diced carrots
1/2 cup diced celery
1 potato, peeled and diced
2 teaspoons salt
2 cups boiling water
2 8-ounce bottles clam juice
1/8 teaspoon saffron
1 28-ounce can Italian plum tomatoes
1 teaspoon thyme
1/4 teaspoon red pepper flakes
1/2 cup chopped fresh parsley
2 bay leaves
1 tablespoon tomato paste
2 cups chopped clams

1. In a Dutch oven, sauté pancetta for 5 minutes. Add garlic, scallions and leeks and cook for a further 5 minutes.

2. Mix in green peppers, carrots, celery, potato, salt, water, clam juice and saffron. Cover, bring to boil, reduce heat and simmer 10 minutes. Stir in tomatoes, herbs, spices and tomato paste. Remove 1 cup of soup mixture and purée until smooth. Return to pot, add clams and stir. Cover and simmer for 15–20 minutes, stirring once or twice. Serve.

Serving suggestion: Serve with Italian bread (page 200) or Baltimore cheese bread (page 203).

*Available at Italian food stores.

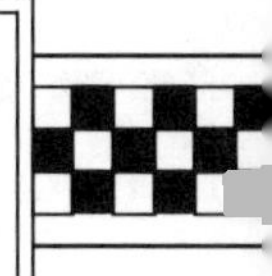

Chicken Stock

From Lexington Market ***Yields about 2 1/2 quarts***

Save up your chicken bones to use when you make a chicken stock. Freeze the bones and defrost when ready to use. Chicken stock also freezes well.

3–4 pounds chicken bones (necks and backs)
3 celery stalks, cut into 1 or 2 pieces
3 carrots, cut into thick slices
3 leeks, cleaned and sliced
2 bay leaves
3 sprigs parsley
10 whole black peppercorns

1. In a large stockpot, combine all the ingredients and cover with cold water. Bring to a boil slowly, uncovered.
2. Lower heat and simmer uncovered for 2–3 hours.
3. Strain through a colander or strainer lined with cheesecloth. Let cool and refrigerate. Skim off any fat from surface and discard. Keep in refrigerator until needed.

Salads

Mount Vernon

Mount Vernon is a neighborhood four blocks square surrounding the site of the first Washington Monument. It is characterized by rows of brownstones in varying architectural designs and with a growing number of charming shops and boutiques.

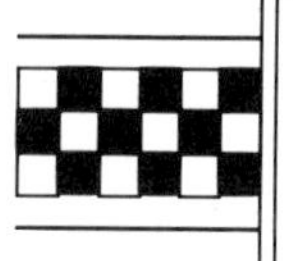

Szechuan Cold Noodles

From Waverly **Chinese** ***Serves 4***

If fresh noodles are used, they require less cooking time (about 3 minutes) than dried noodles. This recipe can be prepared in advance and has a lively taste. A great party or picnic dish.

1/2 cup peanuts, chopped
1/2 cup soy sauce*
2 tablespoons chopped garlic
1 tablespoon chopped ginger
1/2 teaspoon chili oil*
1 teaspoon sugar
2 scallions, chopped (white part only)
1 pound dried thin Chinese egg noodles* or vermicelli
1 tablespoon sesame oil*
1 whole cooked chicken breast, boned, skinned and thinly sliced
2 tomatoes, thinly sliced
1 cucumber, thinly sliced

1. In a bowl, combine peanuts, soy sauce, garlic, ginger, chili oil, sugar and scallions. Mix well. Reserve.

2. In a large saucepan, bring water to a boil, add noodles and cook uncovered for about 10 minutes. Drain and rinse under warm water. Place in a bowl and toss with sesame oil.

3. Place noodles on a serving platter and arrange chicken slices, tomatoes and cucumbers around the noodles. Pour reserved peanut sauce evenly over top. Serve at room temperature.

*Available at Oriental grocery stores.

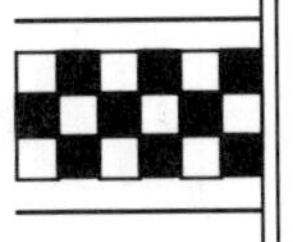

Roasted Red Peppers

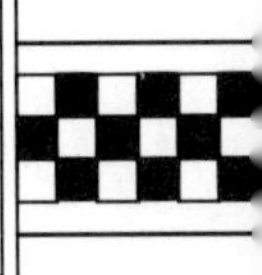

From Canton **Italian** ***Serves 4***

Peppers are available in various colors; try using different peppers to create a very spectacular presentation of this dish.

4 red bell peppers
2 garlic cloves, sliced
2 teaspoons chopped Italian parsley
1/4 teaspoon oregano
Salt and freshly ground pepper to taste
1/4 cup olive oil

1. Broil bell peppers until skin is charred on all sides. Remove and place immediately into a paper bag, seal and let sit for 20–30 minutes. Remove peppers from bag, peel off blackened skin, remove seeds and slice into thin strips. (An alternative method to roast peppers is to cut peppers in half and remove seeds and core. Rub peppers with olive oil, place in pan, skin side up, and roast at 350° for about 10–15 minutes. Remove, cool slightly and peel.)
2. Place peppers in a bowl, add remaining ingredients, mix and allow to marinate for several hours or overnight. Serve.

Serving suggestion: Serve with Italian bread (page 200).

Variation: To serve as an appetizer or first course, lightly brush thin slices of Italian bread with olive oil, toast and place strips of peppers on top.

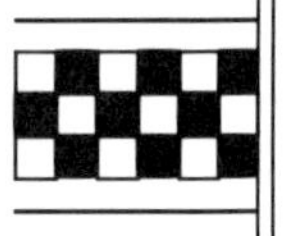

Tarragon Chicken Salad

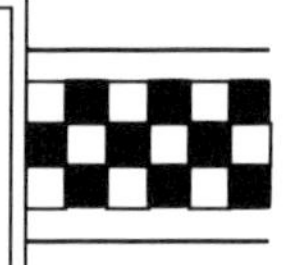

From Washington Hill ***Serves 4***

A classic sauce combined with a tarragon reduction gives an unusual mellow flavor to this refreshing and lovely salad.

2 whole chicken breasts, skinned and boned
Salt and pepper to taste
Pinch of garlic powder
1 cup chicken broth
1 celery stalk, diced
1 scallion, chopped
1 cup seedless grapes
1 cup diced fresh pineapple

TARRAGON REDUCTION
1 teaspoon dried tarragon
1/2 teaspoon chopped shallots
1 teaspoon chopped parsley
Salt and pepper to taste
2 tablespoons tarragon vinegar
2 tablespoons white wine

HOLLANDAISE
1 egg yolk
4 tablespoons unsalted butter
Juice of 1/2 lemon

1. Preheat oven to 350°.
2. Place chicken breasts in a baking dish, season with salt, pepper and garlic powder. Pour in chicken broth and bake for 30 minutes or until just cooked. Cool, dice and reserve.
3. Make tarragon reduction. In a small saucepan, add all ingredients, bring to a boil, lower heat and reduce to 1 tablespoon. Reserve.
4. Make hollandaise. Place all ingredients in the top of a double boiler, bring water to a boil, reduce heat and stir constantly until thickened. Remove from heat.
5. Add tarragon reduction to the hollandaise and mix well.

6. In a large salad bowl or platter, add the chicken, celery, scallions, grapes and pineapple. Pour the tarragon/hollandaise sauce on top to bind and toss gently. Serve at room temperature.

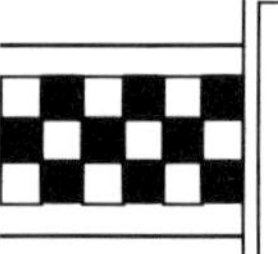

Summer Chicken Salad

From Mt. Washington/Cheswolde ***Serves 6–8***

This resembles a chef's salad and is best made well in advance so that the flavors are well incorporated when salad is served.

2 cups mixed torn greens (iceberg lettuce, curly endive and romaine)
6 tablespoons mayonnaise
1 large purple onion, thinly sliced, separated into rings
1 1/2 teaspoons sugar
Salt and pepper to taste
1 cup diced Swiss cheese
2 cups diced cooked chicken
1 1/2 cups cooked peas
6 slices cooked bacon, crumbled (garnish)
1 cup croutons (garnish)

---

1. In a bowl, toss the greens together.
2. In another bowl, mix together the onion rings, sugar, salt and pepper.
3. In a large salad bowl, place 1/3 of the greens. Spoon in 2 tablespoons mayonnaise. Top with 1/3 of the onions and add 1/3 of the cheese, chicken and peas. Repeat layers twice. Do not toss. Cover and chill at least 2 hours before serving.
4. When ready to serve, top with bacon and croutons.

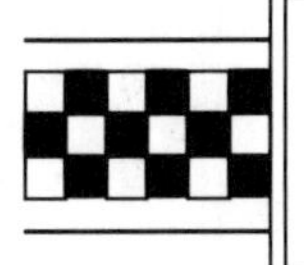

Sunomono (Vinegared Seafood Salad)

From Charles Center **Japanese** ***Serves 4***

Wakame is a seaweed and is sold in its dry state. When soaked and softened it returns to its natural green color. It is also very nutritious and is sometimes used in miso soup.

DRESSING
1/2 cup rice vinegar*
1 tablespoon Japanese soy sauce*
2 tablespoons sugar
3 tablespoons sake* or dry sherry
1/2 teaspoon salt

1 packet dried wakame seaweed*
1 seedless cucumber, preferably unwaxed, thinly sliced
8 large shrimp
1 cup lump crabmeat

1. Prepare dressing. In a saucepan, combine all ingredients and heat until sugar has dissolved. Remove from heat and chill.
2. In a large bowl, place wakame, cover with warm water and soak for 30 minutes to rehydrate. Rinse thoroughly under cold water, pat dry, remove any tough stems and chop into 1-inch pieces.
3. Peel cucumber if waxed and seed if necessary. Soak in salted water for 15 minutes, drain and squeeze excess moisture from cucumber.
4. Peel and devein shrimp. In a saucepan, bring water to a boil, reduce heat, cook shrimp gently for about 3 minutes and drain.
5. On individual serving plates, decoratively arrange wakame, cucumber, shrimp and crabmeat. Pour a little dressing over each salad. Serve at room temperature.

*Available at Oriental or health food shops.

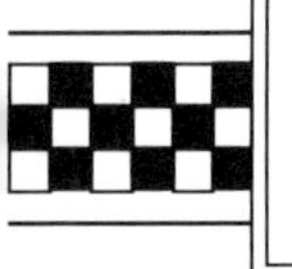

Shrimp Salad

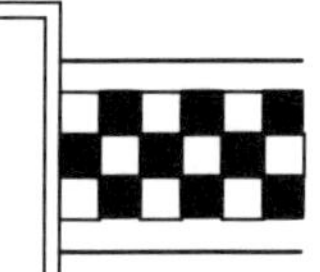

From Govans ***Serves 4***

A light, refreshing salad that has a slight bite to it.

1 pound medium shrimp
1/2 cup chopped celery
2 scallions, chopped (use green part also)
1/2 red bell pepper, chopped
1 teaspoon Worcestershire sauce
1 teaspoon dry mustard
1/4 teaspoon lemon pepper
1/4 teaspoon paprika
1/2 teaspoon Old Bay seasoning
1 teaspoon celery salt
1 tablespoon chopped dill
1–2 tablespoons mayonnaise
1 teaspoon lemon juice
Lettuce leaves
2 hard-cooked eggs, halved (garnish)

1. In a saucepan, bring water to a boil, reduce heat, add shrimp and cook gently for about 5 minutes. Drain, cool, peel and devein.
2. In a bowl, add shrimp and combine remaining ingredients except for eggs and lettuce. Refrigerate for at least 30 minutes.
3. On a large platter, line with lettuce leaves, place shrimp mixture on top and garnish with eggs. Serve.

Serving suggestion: Excellent with Italian bread (page 200).

Variation: Instead of shrimp, substitute lump crabmeat or poached scallops and proceed as above.

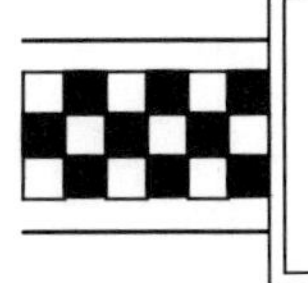

Crab Salad

From Roland Park **Serves 4**

Fresh dill is increasingly easy to find in markets today and is a natural with many fish dishes. Although its flavor is fairly mild, it should be used with a light hand.

- 3 tablespoons mayonnaise
- 3 tablespoons white wine vinegar
- 1 tablespoon dry mustard
- 1/8 teaspoon garlic powder
- 1/8 teaspoon onion powder
- 1 tablespoon chopped fresh (or 1 teaspoon dried) dill
- 1 tablespoon chopped parsley
- 1 head romaine lettuce, washed, patted dry, leaves separated
- 1 pound lump crabmeat, picked through for cartilage
- 4 hard-boiled eggs, quartered (garnish)

1. In a bowl, mix together all ingredients except crabmeat and eggs.
2. Line four individual plates with lettuce and divide crabmeat between them. Pour some of the dressing over each and garnish with hard-boiled eggs. Serve.

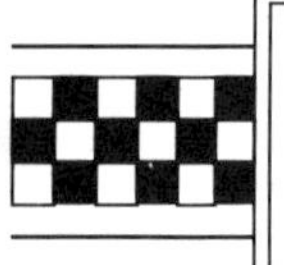

Tzatziki (Cucumber/Yogurt Salad)

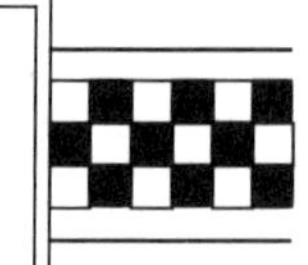

From Highlandtown **Greek** ***Makes about 3 cups***

Yogurt has a slightly tart flavor which enhances this dish. If you have the opportunity to buy freshly made Greek yogurt, you will find the flavor a little more creamy.

2 cucumbers
1 teaspoon salt
2 cups yogurt
1 teaspoon vinegar
2 garlic cloves, minced
2 tablespoons chopped fresh dill
2 tablespoons olive oil, for sprinkling
Romaine lettuce leaves (garnish)

1. Peel and halve cucumbers, sprinkle with salt and let stand 5–10 minutes. Pat dry with paper towel.
2. Shred cucumber into a bowl. Add remaining ingredients except for olive oil and stir until well blended. Cover and refrigerate for several hours.
3. When ready to serve, sprinkle with olive oil and mix to combine. Arrange lettuce leaves on serving plates, top with cucumber/yogurt mixture and serve.

Serving suggestions: Serve as a first course with roast stuffed chicken (page 68) or Greek meatballs (page 62).

Variation: Can be used as a dip with warmed pita bread or served with fried eggplant.

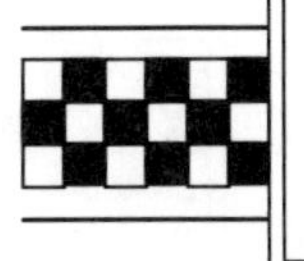

Warmer Krautsalat (Hot Cabbage Salad)

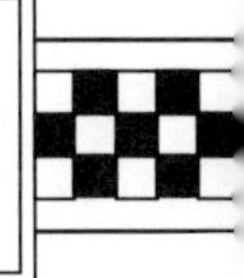

From Patterson Park **German** ***Serves 4–6***

This can be served as a first-course salad or as a vegetable side dish with grilled or roast meat. The success of this easy salad depends on the bacon and vinegar being very hot when poured over the cabbage.

1 head white or red cabbage, finely shredded, washed and well drained
Salt
Boiling water
4 slices bacon, diced
1/4 cup red wine vinegar
Pepper to taste
1/4 teaspoon caraway seed

1. Place drained cabbage in a large bowl, sprinkle with a little salt, cover completely with boiling water, cover bowl and let stand 1 hour.
2. In a skillet, fry bacon until crisp.
3. In a small saucepan, heat vinegar until hot.
4. Drain cabbage and place in a bowl or on individual plates. Pour hot vinegar over cabbage. Season with salt, pepper and caraway seeds. Add bacon and drizzle with hot bacon fat. Serve at once.

Serving suggestion: A wonderful accompaniment for grilled veal chop (page 67) or roast pork shoulder (page 86).

Meat and Fowl

Inner Harbor

Inner Harbor is bound by Pratt Street on the north and leads into Federal Hill on the south. Over the last few years, this area has undergone a rejuvenating change. It's now bustling with activity and tourists anxious to experience the many food stalls, restaurants, shops, and of course the famous National Aquarium.

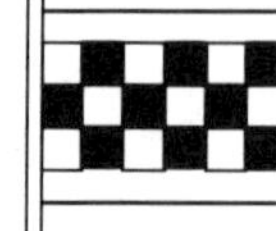

Roast Prime Rib of Beef

From Union Square **Serves 6**

When purchasing prime rib, have the butcher chine the bone for easy carving.

5–6-pound first-cut prime rib
1/2 teaspoon garlic powder
1/2 teaspoon dry mustard
1/2 teaspoon thyme
Salt and freshly ground pepper to taste
1 cup water
1 bay leaf
2 tablespoons cold water mixed with 1 tablespoon flour

1. Preheat oven to 325°.
2. Place beef rib on a rack in a roasting pan. Score fat in a crisscross pattern and season with garlic powder, dry mustard, thyme, salt and pepper. Pour in 1 cup water and add bay leaf.
3. Roast uncovered to desired doneness, approximately 25 minutes per pound for rare, 30 minutes for medium and 40 minutes for well done. If using a thermometer: 140° for rare, 160° for medium and 170° for well done. During cooking, add additional water to pan as needed.
4. When roast is cooked, remove to carving board. Skim excess fat from pan juices and place pan juices on top of stove. Add a little more water if needed and bring to a boil. Reduce heat to simmer and very slowly add the water and flour mixture, stirring constantly, until thickened. Adjust salt and pepper to taste.
5. Slice beef and serve with pan gravy.

Roast Beef Brisket

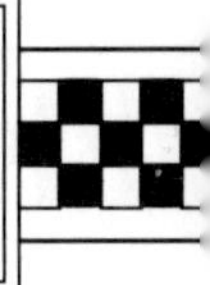

From Corned Beef Row **Jewish** ***Serves 4***

Leftover brisket makes excellent sandwiches spread with horse-radish.

3-pound brisket
1/2 teaspoon garlic powder
1/2 teaspoon paprika
Salt and black pepper to taste
2 onions, coarsely chopped
4 celery stalks, cut into 2-inch pieces
4 carrots, cut into 2-inch pieces
1/2 cup ketchup

1. Preheat oven to 350°.
2. Rub both sides of brisket with the garlic powder, paprika, salt and pepper.
3. In the bottom of a roasting pan, place approximately three-quarters of the chopped vegetables; lay brisket, fat side up on top of vegetables; Add remaining vegetables on top of brisket. Pour 1/4 cup of the ketchup on top of brisket and season with some additional paprika.
4. Fill pan with enough cold water to come halfway up the brisket. Cook brisket for 1 hour, then turn and cook for an additional 1–1 1/2 hours, or until fork-tender.
5. Remove from oven and place roasting pan on top of stove. Add remaining 1/4 cup ketchup to gravy and season with salt and pepper to taste. Simmer for about 10–15 minutes.
6. Slice brisket to desired thickness and serve with pan juices.

Serving suggestion: Serve with plain mashed potatoes and green peas.

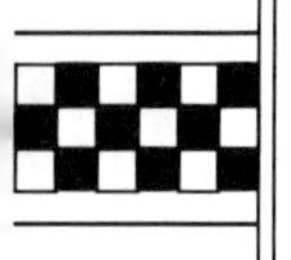

Sauerbraten

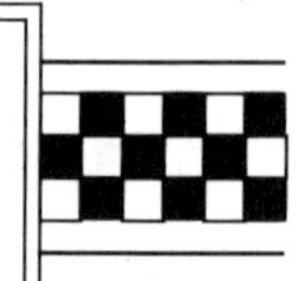

From Patterson Park **German** ***Serves 4***

The ingredients used for the marinade and the length of time the beef marinates give this dish its distinctly tangy flavor and tenderness.

3 pounds beef rump roast

MARINADE

1 1/2 cups red wine vinegar
1 1/2 cups water
1 large onion, sliced
1/2 lemon, sliced
6 whole cloves
2 bay leaves
10 black peppercorns
1 teaspoon salt
1 tablespoon sugar
Flour for dredging beef
2 tablespoons unsalted butter

1. Place meat in a deep bowl. Combine marinade ingredients, pour over meat, cover and refrigerate for 24 hours, turning the meat occasionally in the marinade.
2. Remove meat, strain marinade and reserve. Dust meat lightly with flour.
3. Heat butter in a Dutch oven and brown the meat on all sides. Add 1 cup of the reserved marinade mixture, cover tightly and cook over low heat on top of stove for approximately 2 1/2–3 hours, or until meat is fork-tender. If liquid evaporates during cooking, add a little more of the reserved marinade.
4. Slice and serve with some of the pan juices.

Serving suggestion: Serve with red cabbage (page 160) and dumplings (page 146).

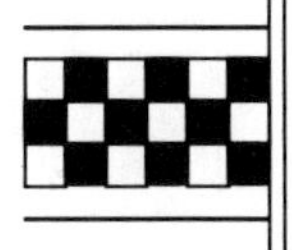

Bigos (Hunter's Stew)

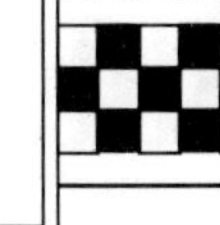

From Broadway Market, Fells Point **Polish** ***Serves 6–8***

Bigos is a traditional Polish stew which varies from kitchen to kitchen. It always consists of a variety of meats and, during the hunting season, the addition of game. Bigos is a very hearty stew and improves in flavor if made 2–3 days ahead. If venison is unavailable, make up the quantity with extra veal, pork or lamb.

1 1/4 pounds boned veal shoulder in one piece
1 1/4 pounds boned pork shoulder in one piece
1 1/4 pounds boned leg of lamb in one piece
3/4 pound venison in one piece
4 carrots, chopped
4 celery stalks, chopped
3 onions, chopped
3 tablespoons chopped parsley
2 cups water
2 32-ounce bags of sauerkraut, rinsed and drained
1/4 pound ham, cut in chunks
1 pound mixed sausages (kielbasa, bratwurst or venison), cut into 1 1/2-inch rounds
2 apples, peeled, cored and diced
2 cups chicken or beef stock
1/2 pound dried Polish mushrooms or dried imported mushrooms, soaked in warm water for 30 minutes
1 cup Madeira or red wine
8 juniper berries
1/2 tablespoon caraway seeds
2 bay leaves

1. Preheat oven to 325°.
2. Place veal, pork, lamb and venison in roasting pan and sprinkle with salt and pepper. Add carrots, celery, onions and parsley to pan and pour in water. Bake for 1 hour, adding a little more water if liquid evaporates.

Remove meat from pan and when cooled cut into 1-inch pieces.

3. Return meat to roasting pan with the vegetables and add remaining ingredients. Return to oven and bake a further 1 1/2–2 hours, or until meat is fork-tender, adding more stock if necessary to prevent sticking. There should be enough liquid left to form a light sauce over the meat. To reheat stew, preheat oven to 325° and bake for about 40–50 minutes, or until well heated through, adding more liquid if necessary.

Serving suggestion: Serve with mustards and horseradish sauce (page 186), together with whole wheat or rye bread and a glass of chilled vodka.

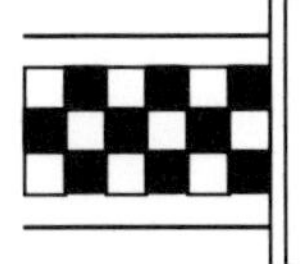

Oven Beef Stew

From Highlandtown ***Serves 4***

This stew freezes beautifully. To reheat, defrost in refrigerator and heat in oven. A good hearty stew for a cold winter's night.

1 1/2 pounds chuck, cut into cubes
1 large onion, coarsely chopped
2 celery stalks, chopped
Salt and pepper to taste
1 tablespoon flour
1 1/2 cups beef broth
4 potatoes, peeled and quartered
4 carrots, peeled and sliced
1/2 teaspoon paprika

1. Preheat oven to 350°.
2. In a 4-quart casserole, layer beef, onions and celery. Season with salt and pepper. Sprinkle with flour (to thicken gravy). Pour in beef broth and bake 1 hour. Remove from oven and add potatoes and carrots. Season with paprika. Cover and bake 1 hour longer, or until potatoes are cooked. Serve.

Serving suggestion: Serve with crusty Italian bread (page 200).

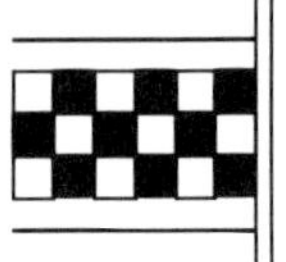

Sukinabe (Beef and Vegetable Stew)

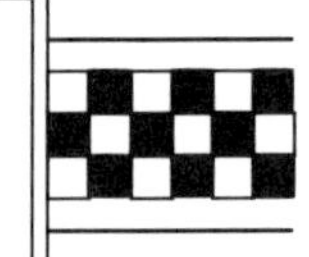

From Charles Center **Japanese** ***Serves 4***

To slice beef paper-thin easily, freeze it for approximately 45 minutes to 1 hour. The Japanese fish stock can be purchased in a granulated instant form and is made by mixing with water. Shiratake are noodle-like threads made from plant starch.

SAUCE
3 cups Japanese fish stock*
1 cup Japanese soy sauce*
1 cup mirin* (Japanese cooking wine)
1–2 tablespoons sugar

2 pounds sirloin, thinly sliced
2 tablespoons peanut oil
1 medium onion, sliced
1 bunch scallions, cut into 1-inch pieces
1 pound hakusai (Napa cabbage), washed and cut into pieces about 2 inches wide
4 shiitake mushrooms, cleaned and quartered
4 pieces tofu, cut into 1-inch cubes
8 ounces shiratake noodles,* sliced into 10-inch lengths

1. Prepare the sauce. Combine all ingredients in a non-reactive bowl and set aside.
2. Heat the oil in a large, deep-sided skillet or wok. Brown the beef quickly and push to one side of the pan.
3. Add onions, scallions and Napa cabbage, taking care to keep each ingredient separate in the skillet.
4. Pour the prepared sauce into the skillet, add the mushrooms, tofu and noodles, again keeping the ingredients separate.

5. Simmer until tofu and noodles are heated and vegetables are cooked, about 10 minutes. Serve directly from cooking pan.

*Available at Oriental specialty stores.

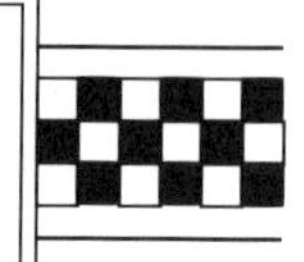

Corned Beef and Cabbage

From Locust Point **Irish** ***Serves 6–8***

A traditional dish to serve on St. Patrick's Day. To add a little zest, serve with your favorite mustard.

3–3 1/2-pound corned beef brisket
Water
2 large onions, peeled and quartered
4 carrots, cut into 2-inch pieces
4 celery stalks, chopped
4 potatoes, peeled and quartered
1 small head of cabbage, quartered

1. Place brisket in a large stockpot and cover with cold water. Bring to a boil, reduce heat, cover and simmer 3–3 1/2 hours, or until tender. Remove to platter.
2. To the stockpot liquid, add the onions, carrots, celery and potatoes and simmer approximately 40–50 minutes. Add cabbage, cover and cook about 20 minutes, or until vegetables are tender.
3. Return corned beef to stockpot and simmer until heated through.
4. Remove corned beef and slice against the grain. Place slices on a serving platter along with all the vegetables and a little of the broth to moisten. Serve.

Serving suggestion: Serve with beaten biscuits (page 202).

Stir-Fried Flank Steak with Snowpeas, Scallions and Mushrooms

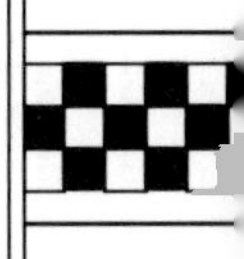

From Morrell Park **Chinese** ***Serves 4***

Fresh ginger is a tuberous root. One way of preserving fresh ginger is to store it in a jar covered with dry sherry or gin and refrigerate. Use as necessary. Dried ginger is not a substitute for fresh ginger in recipes as it has a sweeter flavor and is generally used in dessert dishes.

1 1/2–2-pound flank steak

MARINADE
1 tablespoon dry sherry
1 tablespoon red wine vinegar
3 tablespoons soy sauce
1/2 teaspoon sugar
1 teaspoon arrowroot

5 tablespoons peanut oil
4 slices fresh ginger
1/4 pound snowpeas
2 scallions, trimmed and cut into 1-inch lengths
1/4 pound fresh mushrooms, cleaned and sliced

1. Place flank steak in freezer for about 1 hour until semi-frozen. With a very sharp knife, cut lengthwise down middle and then slice very thinly across the grain.
2. In a bowl, combine sherry, vinegar, soy sauce, sugar and arrowroot.
3. Place meat in marinade for at least 30 minutes.
4. In a large skillet or wok, add 3 tablespoons of the peanut oil and heat over a high flame. Sauté ginger for 30 seconds, then remove and discard ginger.
5. To the hot oil, add the snowpeas and stir-fry until tender but crisp. Remove snowpeas and reserve.
6. Add scallions and another tablespoon of oil, if needed, and stir-fry 1 minute. Add mushrooms and stir-fry 1 minute longer. Remove onions and mushrooms and reserve.

7. Add remaining tablespoon of oil, add meat and marinade and stir-fry 3–5 minutes. Do not overcook steak. Return vegetables to skillet or wok and stir-fry quickly until just heated through.

Serving suggestion: Serve over plain steamed rice.

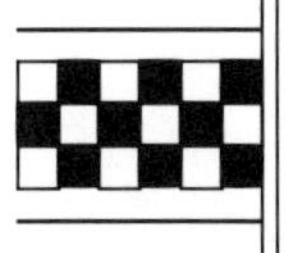

Beef with Snowpeas

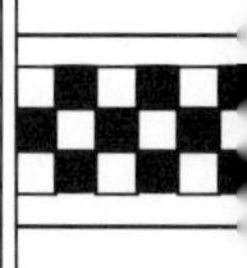

From Waverly **Chinese** ***Serves 4***

The combination of egg white, cornstarch and soy sauce helps tenderize the beef. For this particular dish it's very important not to overcook the beef or it becomes chewy and tough. Cooking until medium rare ensures a juicy and tender morsel of meat.

1 egg white, lightly beaten
1/2 teaspoon cornstarch
1/4 cup soy sauce
Pinch of sugar
1 pound London broil, thinly sliced
1 tablespoon peanut oil
1/4 pound snowpeas, trimmed

1. In a large bowl, mix together the egg white, cornstarch, soy sauce and sugar. Whisk until smooth. Add beef and marinate for 20–30 minutes. Drain and reserve marinade.

2. In a wok or skillet, heat about 1 tablespoon of oil until hot. Stir-fry snowpeas for 10 seconds. Add beef and quickly cook until just seared, about 1–2 minutes. Add marinade and stir-fry a few seconds to heat. Serve.

Serving suggestion: Serve with white rice and stir-fried bok choy (page 164) or kim chee (page 161).

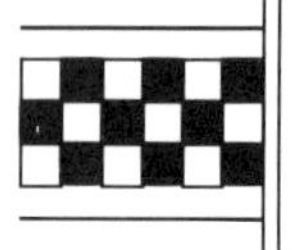

Bul-Go-Gi (Barbecued Beef)

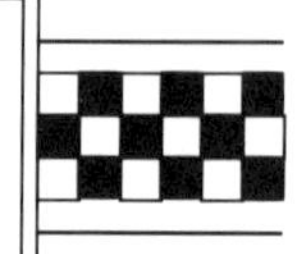

From Upton **Korean** ***Serves 4***

This is an easy dish that makes excellent use of any leftover beef. The recipe calls for sweet soy sauce which is thicker, darker looking in color, and has a sweeter taste than regular soy sauce.

1 tablespoon rice wine or white wine vinegar
1 teaspoon sugar
2 garlic cloves, minced
Pinch of salt
1/3 cup sweet soy sauce*
2 scallions, chopped
Black pepper to taste
1 pound cooked beef, thinly sliced
2 tablespoons peanut oil

1. In a bowl, mix together vinegar, sugar, garlic, salt, soy sauce, scallions and black pepper. Add beef and marinate 1–2 hours.
2. Drain beef and reserve marinade.
3. Heat oil in a skillet or wok and quickly stir-fry the beef. Add a little of the marinade and cook 1–2 minutes.
4. Serve at once.

Serving suggestion: Serve with plain white or brown rice and cold noodles (page 35).

*Available at Oriental or specialty stores.

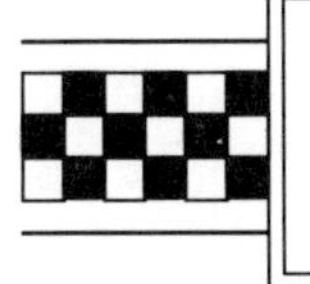

Meatloaf

From Hampden ***Serves 4***

If you buy fresh horseradish, grate and use as is. To keep fresh, put it in a jar and cover with white vinegar and a little salt.

1 1/2 pounds lean ground beef
1/4 pound lean ground pork
2 eggs, beaten
1 medium onion, minced
1 teaspoon fresh horseradish
1/2 teaspoon dry mustard
1/2 teaspoon thyme
1/4 teaspoon garlic powder
1 tablespoon chopped fresh parsley
Salt and pepper to taste
1/4 cup breadcrumbs
1 chicken or beef bouillon cube
1/4 pound mushrooms, sliced
2 tablespoons water combined with 1 tablespoon flour for thickening

1. Preheat oven to 375°.
2. In a bowl, mix meatloaf ingredients. Shape into a loaf and place in a buttered roasting pan. Add bouillon cube and chopped mushrooms to pan. Cover and bake for 1 hour.
3. When cooked, remove loaf from roasting pan and place pan on top of stove. Add about 1/3 cup of water to pan juices and bring to a boil. Reduce heat to low and slowly stir in the water/flour mixture. Simmer to desired thickness. (Additional water may be added to pan to thin gravy if needed.)
4. Slice meatloaf and serve with pan gravy.

Serving suggestion: Serve with mashed potatoes and a salad.

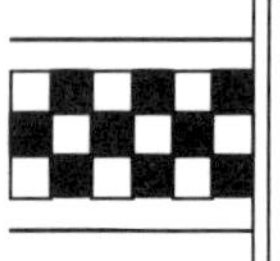

Meatloaf Surprise

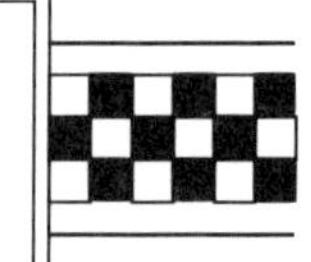

From Northeast Baltimore ***Serves 6–8***

What a delicious surprise to slice the meatloaf and find it oozing with Cheddar cheese. Any leftovers will make terrific sandwiches.

2 pounds ground beef
1 small onion, minced
1 green bell pepper, minced
1/4 cup breadcrumbs
1 egg
1/2 teaspoon oregano
1/4 teaspoon garlic powder
Salt and pepper to taste
4 ounces extra sharp Cheddar, thinly sliced
5–6 slices bacon
1 large tomato, sliced

1. Preheat oven to 350°.
2. Combine ground beef, onion, peppers, breadcrumbs, egg, oregano, garlic powder, salt and pepper and mix thoroughly.
3. Divide the meat and place half the mixture in a shallow casserole or pie plate, forming it into a round. With your fingers pat the center, making a well and leaving a rim around the edges. Fill with the cheese slices and top with the remaining meat mixture, sealing the edges with your fingers to enclose the cheese.
4. Lay bacon slices over loaf and top with sliced tomatoes. Place in oven and bake for 1 hour, or until done.

Serving suggestion: Serve with potato pancakes (page 144).

Variation: Instead of ground beef, make the meatloaf using lean ground turkey.

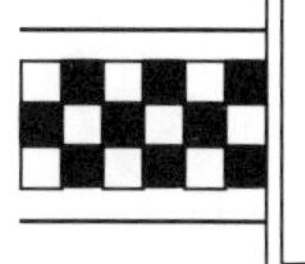

Keftethes (Baked Meatballs)

From Locust Point **Greek** ***Serves 4***

Use fresh mint when available. However, if you use dried mint the rule of thumb is use half as much dried as fresh because dried is more concentrated.

1 pound ground beef
1/2 cup milk
2–3 garlic cloves, minced
1 small onion, grated
2 tablespoons minced fresh mint leaves
2 eggs, well beaten
Salt and pepper to taste

SAUCE
2–3 tablespoons unsalted butter
Juice of 1 lemon
Oregano to taste
Water

1. Preheat oven to 350°.
2. To make meatballs, mix all the ingredients together thoroughly and form into 1-inch balls.
3. Line a jelly-roll pan with aluminum foil and place meatballs on top. Bake for approximately 25 minutes or until meatballs are cooked through. Place in a bowl and keep warm.
4. To make the sauce, melt butter in a skillet over low heat and whisk in the lemon juice. Sprinkle with oregano and add about a tablespoon of water. Bring mixture to a boil and whisk for about 1 minute. Remove from heat and pour over meatballs. Serve at once.

Serving suggestion: Serve with boiled greens.

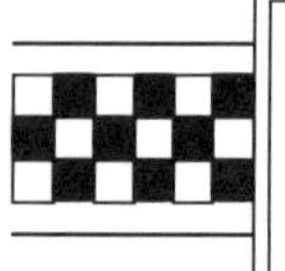

Stuffed Veal Roast

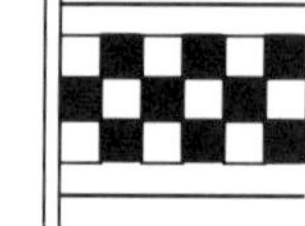

From Broadway Market, Fells Point **Serves 4**

Veal breast is perfect for stuffing and a special way to enjoy veal without paying high prices. Covering the veal during cooking ensures that it will be moist and tender.

1 1/2 pounds ground veal
1/2 green pepper, diced
1/2 red pepper, diced
2 tablespoons chopped parsley
4 pounds veal breast, boned
Salt and white pepper to taste
2 teaspoons basil
2 cups white wine

1. Preheat oven to 350°.
2. In a bowl, combine the ground veal, peppers and parsley.
3. Lay the veal breast flat on a counter and season with salt, pepper and basil.
4. Spread the veal mixture down one side of the breast. Roll tightly and tie with string.
5. Place on a rack in roasting pan and pour 2 cups white wine over veal. Roast uncovered for 35 minutes. Cover and continue cooking another 1 1/2 hours, or until tender. (Veal roasts should be cooked approximately 35 minutes per pound.)

Serving suggestion: Serve with brown rice or rice pilaf (page 181).

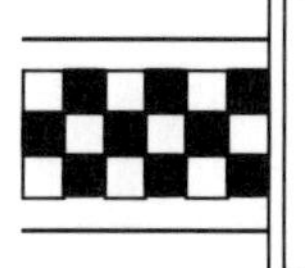

Oven-Baked Veal Stew

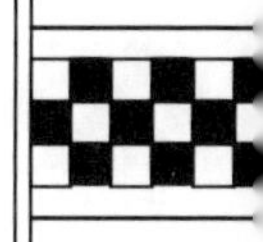

From Cross Street Market, Federal Hill ***Serves 4***

This veal stew, as with most stews, can be made ahead. Reheat over low heat for 10–15 minutes, or until meat and vegetables are warmed through. Some additional warm water may be needed if pan juices are not sufficient.

2 onions, sliced
2 pounds veal cubes
1/4 cup soy sauce
Pinch of black pepper
1 teaspoon paprika
2 tablespoons flour
1 1/2 cups chicken broth
2 medium potatoes, peeled and quartered
3 large carrots, sliced into 1/2-inch rings
2 celery stalks, cut into 1-inch pieces

1. Preheat oven to 350°.
2. In a 3-quart Dutch oven or casserole, place a layer of onions. Arrange meat on top of onions and add soy sauce. Sprinkle pepper, paprika and flour over the meat. Pour in chicken broth, cover and braise in oven for 1 hour.
3. Add potatoes, carrots and celery and cook covered another hour, or until vegetables and meat are tender.

Serving suggestion: Serve with Italian bread (page 200).

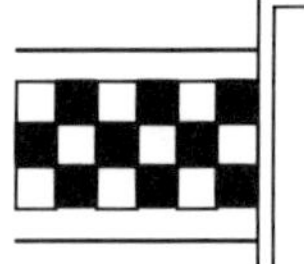

Vitello in Vino Blanca (Veal in White Wine Sauce)

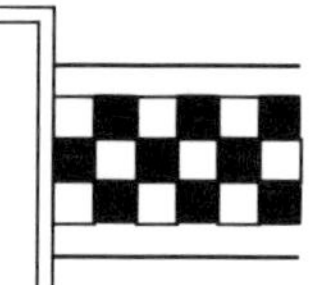

From Little Italy **Italian** ***Serves 4***

Cook veal very briefly until still pink in the center; overcooking toughens the meat and can ruin this beautiful dish.

1 cup flour
1/2 teaspoon garlic powder
4 tablespoons butter
2 tablespoons olive oil
1 1/2 pounds veal scaloppini, pounded to 1/4-inch thickness
4 scallions, minced
1/2 pound mushrooms, sliced
1 cup dry white wine
1/4 cup fresh chopped parsley
Salt and pepper to taste

1. On a plate, season flour with garlic powder and set aside.
2. In a skillet, heat butter and olive oil. Dredge scaloppini in flour and brown quickly on both sides until just cooked, 1–2 minutes. Remove and keep warm.
3. Add scallions and mushrooms to skillet and sauté 1 minute. Add wine and parsley and cook another minute. Return scaloppini to skillet and heat through gently, turning them in sauce to coat. Season with salt and pepper and serve at once with wine sauce.

Serving suggestion: Serve with rice pilaf (page 181) and a green vegetable.

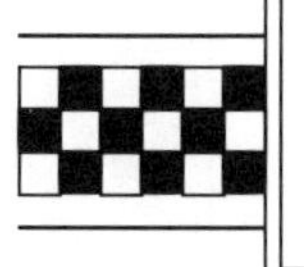

Veal Marsala

From Little Italy **Italian** ***Serves 4***

Marsala is a Sicilian dessert wine and is used in many Italian dishes. The best scaloppini is from the leg. Have the butcher slice the veal against the grain, which will prevent shrinkage or curling around the edges during cooking.

1 tablespoon olive oil
2 tablespoons unsalted butter
Flour for dusting veal, plus 1 tablespoon for sauce
8 veal scaloppini, pounded
1/2 cup Marsala
1/4 cup fresh lemon juice
Fresh parsley (garnish)

1. Put oil and butter into a skillet and heat.
2. Dredge veal lightly with flour and brown quickly in the hot oil/butter mixture for 1–2 minutes on each side. When all the veal is cooked, transfer to a platter and put aside.
3. Add the Marsala to the skillet, scraping the cooking residues loose from bottom of pan. When Marsala is slightly reduced, add lemon juice and stir.
4. With a fork, gradually incorporate the 1 tablespoon of flour into sauce, stirring and whisking to prevent lumping. When smooth and slightly thickened, return veal with any juices from the platter to the pan. Heat through for 30 seconds.
5. Sprinkle with fresh parsley and serve at once.

Serving suggestion: Serve with rice pilaf (page 181) or buttered noodles and a green vegetable.

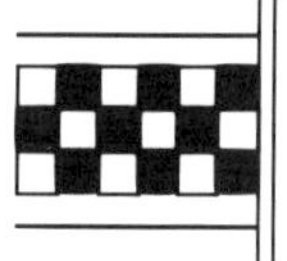

Grilled Veal Chops

From Inner Harbor **Serves 4**

This recipe calls for Herb de Provence, but if it is not available, a similar mixture can be made by combining equal proportions of dried thyme, oregano, savory, rosemary and fennel seed. Chops may also be broiled or barbecued on the outdoor grill.

4 1-inch-thick veal chops
Olive oil
1 tablespoon Herb de Provence
Lemon pepper or freshly ground black pepper to taste

1. Rub veal chops with oil and sprinkle with herbs and pepper. Let stand at least 30 minutes.
2. Preheat oven to 300°.
3. Brush a skillet or ridged grill with a little olive oil and heat until hot. Cook chops for 3 minutes on each side. Transfer chops to an oven-proof baking dish and bake for about 6 minutes for medium rare. Do not overcook or chops will dry out and toughen. Serve.

Serving suggestions: Serve with a side order of pasta with red pepper sauce (page 178) or with zucchini and red bell pepper sauté (page 151) or baked fennel (page 169).

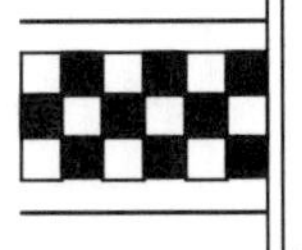

Roast Chicken with Herb Bread Stuffing

From Fells Point ***Serves 4***

Pan-roasted and stuffed is one of the tastiest ways of preparing chicken. It makes a perfect Sunday or special-occasion meal.

3 1/2-pound chicken
Salt and pepper to taste

STUFFING
4–6 tablespoons unsalted butter
1 medium onion, minced
1 cup finely chopped celery
1 chicken liver, minced
1/4 teaspoon sage
1/2 teaspoon marjoram
1/2 teaspoon thyme
2 cups breadcubes
Salt and pepper to taste
1 egg white
Poultry seasoning
Juice of half a lemon
2 tablespoons unsalted butter

1. Rinse chicken inside and out and pat dry thoroughly.
2. To make stuffing, melt butter in skillet over medium heat, add onion and celery and sauté approximately 15 minutes, or until celery is softened. Add minced chicken liver and sauté another 5 minutes. Season with sage, marjoram and thyme and cook 1 minute longer. Place breadcubes in a bowl, toss with onion/celery mixture and season with salt and pepper. Cool slightly. Add egg white and mix to combine.
3. Preheat oven to 350°.
4. Season inside of chicken with poultry seasoning, then stuff and truss.

5. Place chicken in roasting pan, pour on lemon juice and roast uncovered for 15 minutes. Pour 2 tablespoons of melted butter over chicken and continue roasting uncovered for another 1 1/2–1 3/4 hours, or until fully cooked. Chicken should be basted periodically with pan juices. A little water should be added during cooking to prevent pan juices from burning. About 20 minutes before removing from oven, season chicken with salt and freshly ground pepper to taste.

6. Remove chicken from oven and allow to rest 15 minutes before carving. Remove stuffing.

7. For gravy, degrease pan juice and serve along with chicken and stuffing.

Serving suggestion: Serve with your favorite vegetable dish.

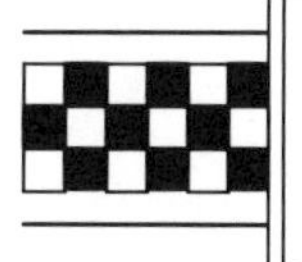

Chicken Dijon

From Broadway Market, Fells Point ***Serves 4***

The Dijon mustard marinade gives this dish a delightfully zesty flavor and results in a tasty, tender sautéed chicken.

1 cup Dijon mustard
1/2 cup white wine or dry vermouth
3–4 large garlic cloves, minced
4 whole chicken breasts, halved, boned, skinned and flattened
2 cups breadcrumbs
8 tablespoons (1 stick) unsalted butter

1. In a bowl large enough to hold the chicken breasts, combine the Dijon mustard, wine and garlic cloves. Add the chicken breasts and marinate for at least 6 hours or overnight.
2. Remove chicken from marinade and coat with breadcrumbs. Refrigerate for 1 hour.
3. In a skillet large enough to hold the chicken breasts comfortably, heat butter until hot and sauté on each side for approximately 7–8 minutes, or until lightly golden and chicken is cooked through. Do not overcook. Serve at once.

Serving suggestion: Serve with rice and a tossed green salad.

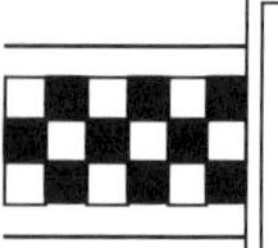

Sautéed Chicken Breasts with White Wine, Lemon and Walnuts

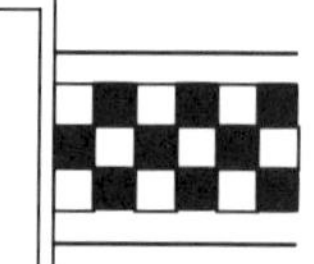

From Charles Village **Serves 4**

This is a lovely, refreshing chicken dish and is wonderful for entertaining a large group of guests. The walnuts, which are added at the very end, lend a unique taste and texture.

4 tablespoons unsalted butter
3 tablespoons olive oil
2 whole chicken breasts, boned, skinned and divided in half
Flour for dredging
1 egg, beaten
2 garlic cloves, minced
1 cup chicken stock
1/4 cup dry white wine or dry vermouth
1 tablespoon soft butter combined with 1 tablespoon flour for thickening
Juice of 1 lemon
Salt and freshly ground pepper to taste
1/2 cup chopped walnuts
2 tablespoons chopped fresh Italian parsley
1 lemon, thinly sliced (garnish)

---

1. In a skillet, heat butter and oil until hot. Dust each piece of chicken with flour and dip in beaten egg. Let excess egg drip off. Slip chicken breasts into hot butter/oil mixture and sauté until lightly golden on each side, about 3 minutes. Remove from pan and set aside.
2. Add garlic to skillet and sauté 1 minute. Add chicken stock, wine and butter/flour mixture and cook until sauce is slightly thickened. Add lemon juice and return chicken to pan, turning in the sauce to coat. Cover and cook approximately 10–15 minutes, or until chicken is just done.
3. Sprinkle with walnuts and parsley and serve garnished with sliced lemon.

Serving suggestion: Serve with rice pilaf (page 181) or potato pancakes (page 144).

Sautéed Chicken and Squash

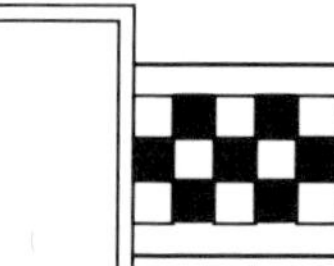

From Morrell Park ***Serves 4***

Here is another chicken recipe to add to your repertoire with the addition of scrumptious squash. The technique of adding the hot tomato sauce to the egg neutralizes the temperature of the egg and prevents it from curdling.

2 cups whole Italian plum tomatoes
1/4 teaspoon sugar
1 bay leaf
1/4 cup olive oil
4 chicken legs, halved
6 large garlic cloves, minced
2 onions, chopped
1 large squash, cut into bite-size pieces (zucchini, summer or bush squash may be used)
1 egg, beaten
2 tablespoons chopped fresh parsley

---

1. Place tomatoes, sugar and bay leaf in a saucepan and cook over medium heat until liquid has evaporated, about 10–15 minutes. During cooking, break tomatoes into pieces with a spatula.
2. Meanwhile, in a Dutch oven or casserole, brown the chicken parts in olive oil, remove chicken to a platter and reserve.
3. Add garlic and onion to the pan in which the chicken was browned and sauté 5 minutes. Add tomato sauce and chicken, cover and cook 20 minutes.
4. Add squash to pan and cook 15 minutes. Remove lid and cook an additional 10 minutes, or until chicken is tender. Remove chicken and squash to serving dish.
5. Add 4–6 tablespoons of the hot tomato mixture to the beaten egg, stirring constantly. Then pour mixture

back into the pan and cook gently 2 minutes. Pour sauce over chicken, garnish with parsley and serve.

Variation: Substitute other vegetables for the squash, such as cooked eggplant.

Maryland Fried Chicken

From Dickeyville ***Serves 4***

This is the traditional way of preparing Maryland fried chicken. For a successful crispy chicken, make sure the oil is hot and kept at a constant temperature.

2 1/2–3-pound frying chicken, cut into parts
Salt and freshly ground pepper to taste
Cayenne pepper to taste
Flour for dredging
Vegetable oil for deep-frying

1. Rinse chicken pieces and pat dry thoroughly. Sprinkle with salt, pepper and cayenne.
2. In a deep fryer with a lid, heat oil until hot. Dredge chicken pieces in flour, shake off excess and place a few pieces at a time into the hot oil. Cover and cook until golden brown, about 7–8 minutes on each side. Drain on paper towels. Serve.

Serving suggestions: Serve with cornbread (page 201) and Southern black-eyed peas (page 165), or mushroom pie (page 166) and baked rutabaga (page 170).

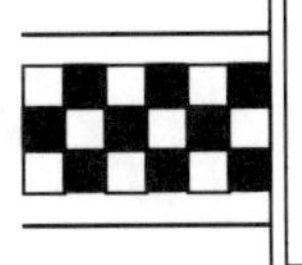

Chicken Tikka Masala (Skewered Chicken Kebabs)

From Charles Center **Indian** ***Serves 4***

A wonderful array of spices are subtly incorporated into this lovely chicken dish. These kebabs can also be served as a first course or as an appetizer with cocktails.

1 pound chicken breasts, boned and skinned
1 teaspoon salt
1 teaspoon chili powder
1 teaspoon paprika
1/2 teaspoon turmeric powder
1/4 cup yogurt
2 garlic cloves, minced
1 1/2-inch slice fresh ginger root, minced
1 teaspoon coriander powder
1 teaspoon cumin powder
1 teaspoon ground cinnamon
1 teaspoon black pepper
1 teaspoon black cardamom powder
2 tablespoons white vinegar
1 1/2 tablespoons lemon juice
2 cups vegetable oil

SAUCE
2–3 tablespoons vegetable oil
1 large onion, minced
4 Italian plum tomatoes, peeled, seeded and chopped
1/4 cup heavy cream or yogurt

1. Cut chicken into 1-inch cubes. Combine remaining ingredients in a bowl, add chicken and marinate 12–24 hours.
2. To make sauce, heat oil in a skillet and fry onions gently, stirring occasionally for about 15 minutes, or until golden brown. Add tomatoes and cook 10–15 minutes. Reserve.
3. Preheat oven to broil.

4. Remove chicken from marinade and place on skewers. Broil approximately 10 minutes, turning chicken occasionally.
5. Reheat sauce, adding the heavy cream or yogurt. Remove chicken pieces from skewers and add to the sauce. Heat gently 1 minute and serve.

Serving suggestion: Serve with Basmati rice (page 180) and palak paneer (page 156).

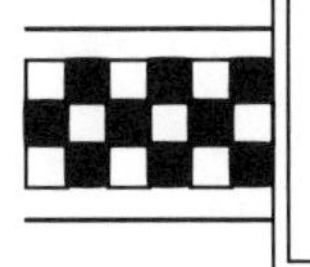

Chicken with Rice

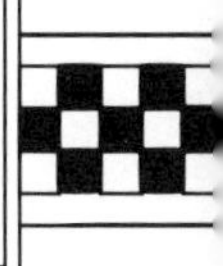

From Edmondson Village **Serves 4**

This is a very tasty chicken dish prepared with only five ingredients.

2 whole chicken breasts, halved
Water
1 cup uncooked rice
1 10 3/4-ounce can onion soup
1 10 3/4-ounce can cream of mushroom soup

1. Preheat oven to 350°.
2. Place chicken breasts in a Dutch oven or casserole and cover with water. Cook in oven for approximately 20 minutes. Remove from oven and allow chicken to cool in broth. When cool, remove skin and meat from the bones and cut into slices. Reserve broth.
3. In a casserole, add rice, cover with onion soup, place chicken pieces on top and cover with mushroom soup together with 2 cups of the reserved broth. Cover and bake approximately 45 minutes, or until rice is done and liquid is absorbed.

Serving suggestion: Serve with a mixed green salad.

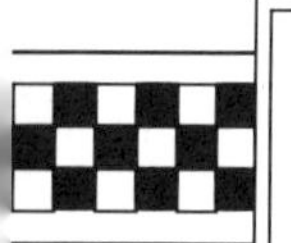

Fricasseed Chicken with Noodles

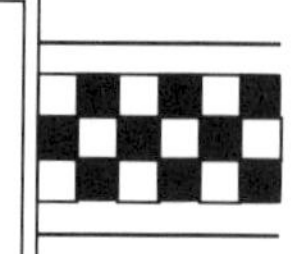

From Mondawmin ***Serves 4***

To clean the leek used in this recipe, slice lengthwise up to the root and rinse thoroughly under cold running water. This dish is light and tasty and can be prepared easily for a large gathering.

4 whole chicken breasts, skinned
1 cup chopped celery
1 leek, sliced
6 cups water
1/2 pound wide egg noodles
1/4 cup flour
1 cup light cream

1. Preheat oven to 350°.
2. In a Dutch oven or casserole, place chicken, celery and leek. Cover with water and place in oven for 20–25 minutes, or until chicken is just cooked. Remove chicken from broth, cool and cut meat from bones in large pieces. Reserve.
3. To the broth, add noodles, cover pan with lid slightly askew and cook on top of stove 20–25 minutes, or until noodles are tender. (Liquid will have reduced slightly.) Set aside.
4. In a small bowl, blend flour with enough broth from pot to form a smooth paste. Stir back into the broth with the noodles and cook over very low heat, whisking constantly until thickened. Add chicken and cream and heat through gently for approximately 10 minutes. Serve.

Serving suggestion: Serve with beaten biscuits (page 202).

Chicken Stew with Biscuits

From Southwest Baltimore ***Serves 4–6***

A hearty winter dish with a delicious light biscuit crust.

1 whole chicken, cut into parts
1 large onion, quartered
2 carrots, cut into 1/2-inch-thick rounds
2 celery stalks, cut into 2-inch pieces
1/8 teaspoon thyme
1 bay leaf
1/2 teaspoon salt
Freshly ground pepper to taste
1 teaspoon lemon juice
1 cup chicken broth
3 chicken bouillon cubes
1 1/2 cups water

BISCUITS
1 cup Bisquick buttermilk mix
1/2 teaspoon garlic powder
Approximately 3–4 tablespoons cold water
3 tablespoons flour mixed with 1/4 cup cold water for thickening

1. Place chicken parts in a Dutch oven together with onions, carrots, celery, thyme, bay leaf, salt, pepper, lemon juice, chicken broth, bouillon cubes and water. Bring to a boil, reduce heat and simmer covered for approximately 40–60 minutes, or until chicken and vegetables are tender.

2. Meanwhile prepare the biscuits. In a bowl, blend together all ingredients until mixture is of the consistency to roll out easily. On a lightly floured work surface, roll out dough to approximately 1/8-inch thickness and cut into 1-inch squares, or cut with a cookie cutter. Drop biscuits into boiling salted water and cook for approximately 15–18 minutes. Remove with slotted spoon and reserve.

3. When chicken and vegetables are cooked, remove with a slotted spoon to a serving dish.
4. To the simmering pan juices add the flour/water mixture, stirring constantly, and cook 1–2 minutes until thickened. Return chicken, vegetables and biscuits to the pot and simmer gently for 10–15 minutes. Serve.

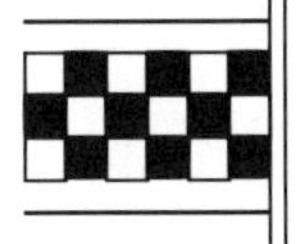

Chicken Pie

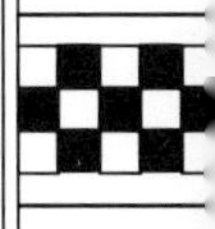

From Patterson Park **Ukrainian** ***Serves 6–8***

A hearty winter dish that is appealing and tasty. The sour cream pastry has a soft, delicate texture that enhances the full-flavored filling.

1 3–3 1/2-pound chicken, cut into parts
Water
1 large onion, halved
1 large celery stalk, halved
1 garlic clove, sliced

SOUR CREAM PASTRY
3 1/2 cups all-purpose flour
1 teaspoon baking powder
1/4 teaspoon salt
1/4 pound butter, chilled
2 eggs, lightly beaten
1 cup sour cream

FILLING
1/2 cup sour cream
3 tablespoons chopped parsley
1/4 teaspoon ground nutmeg
1 tablespoon lemon juice
Salt and white pepper to taste
3 cups cooked rice
1/2 pound mushrooms, sliced
1 tablespoon butter
4 hard-cooked eggs, chopped
1/4 cup chopped fresh dill
1 egg yolk, beaten

1. In a stockpot, combine first four ingredients, add enough water to cover chicken and bring to a boil. Reduce heat and simmer gently uncovered, approximately 1 hour or until chicken is tender. (During cooking skim any residue that rises to the top.) Remove chicken from the stock, take meat from bones and cut into large pieces. Cover chicken pieces and set aside. Reserve stock.
2. To make pastry, combine flour, baking powder and salt in a bowl. Cut butter into dry ingredients until mixture resembles coarse crumbs. Combine beaten eggs with sour cream and slowly add to the coarse crumbs, mixing just until dough forms into a ball. Di-

vide in half. Roll dough out onto a lightly floured surface to 1/8-inch thickness and carefully place into a deep 9-inch pie plate. Reserve remaining dough for top of pie.

3. For filling, in a bowl, combine 1 cup stock and sour cream and set aside. In another bowl, mix together parsley, nutmeg, lemon juice, reserved chicken, salt and pepper.

4. In a skillet, sauté mushrooms in butter until softened. Reserve.

5. To the pie crust add a layer of rice, chicken mixture, sautéed mushrooms, chopped eggs and dill. Continue layering ending with a layer of rice. Pour reserved stock and sour cream mixture evenly over top.

6. Preheat oven to 400°.

7. Roll out the reserved dough and place on top of mixture. Crimp edges to seal and make a slit in center of crust. Brush with egg yolk and bake approximately 15 minutes. Reduce heat to 350° and continue baking for another 30–40 minutes or until crust is nicely golden.

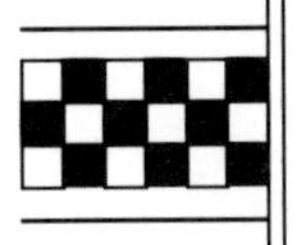

Rolled Stuffed Pork Roast

From Broadway Market, Fells Point ***Serves 6***

The addition of nutmeg and cinnamon gives this stuffing a slightly Middle Eastern flavor. If possible, use Apple Jack instead of apple juice for a more intense flavor.

STUFFING
1 tablespoon butter
1/2 cup diced celery
1/2 cup diced onion
1/2 cup croutons
1/2 cup diced apples
1/8 teaspoon nutmeg
1/8 teaspoon cinnamon
1/4 teaspoon white pepper
1 tablespoon raisins, soaked in hot water for 1/2 hr.
1 tablespoon crushed walnuts
1–2 tablespoons apple juice (just enough to moisten stuffing)

4-pound boneless pork loin, butterflied
1 cup chicken stock
1 cup Apple Jack (apple juice may be substituted)

1. Preheat oven to 325°.
2. To make stuffing, melt butter in a skillet, add celery and onion and sauté for about 5 minutes. Add remaining ingredients and just enough apple juice to moisten mixture.
3. Lay butterflied pork loin on counter. Place stuffing down the middle; do not overstuff. (Remaining stuffing may be cooked separately.) Roll the loin around the stuffing and tie tightly with string.
4. Place in a roasting pan. Pour chicken stock and Apple Jack over the roast and cook uncovered for 1 hour. If liquid evaporates, add a little more stock to pan and

continue cooking, covered, for an additional 35–40 minutes, or until tender. If using a thermometer, it should register 180°.

5. Remove to a serving platter and allow to rest for 5 minutes. Slice and serve.

Serving suggestion: This dish goes well with potato pancakes (page 144) and string beans.

Roast Fresh Pork Shoulder

From Morrell Park ***Serves 4***

Tiger sauce is slightly spicy and adds an interesting flavor to this dish. It can also be added to gravies and sauces.

1 3-pound fresh pork shoulder
1 teaspoon salt
1/2 teaspoon garlic powder
1/4 teaspoon red pepper
1/2 teaspoon fresh ground black pepper
1 teaspoon ground ginger
1 cup water
1 tablespoon cornstarch, mixed with 2 tablespoons cold water
3 tablespoons Tiger sauce

1. Preheat oven to 325°.
2. With a knife score the skin of the pork shoulder in a crisscross pattern.
3. In a bowl, combine salt, garlic powder, red pepper, black pepper and ginger and rub roast all over with spices. Place pork shoulder on a rack, skin side up, in a roasting pan and add 1 cup of water to bottom of pan. Roast uncovered approximately 3 hours, or until thermometer reaches 180°. (During cooking additional water may be needed to prevent drippings from burning.)
4. Remove pork shoulder to serving platter. Place roasting pan on top of stove and skim off fat. Bring drippings to a boil, adding a little more water if necessary and scraping particles adhering to pan. Reduce heat to low and very slowly add cornstarch mixture until thickened. Remove from heat and stir in Tiger sauce.

5. Slice pork shoulder and serve with sauce.

Serving suggestion: Serve with stir-fried bok choy (page 164) or your favorite vegetable dish.

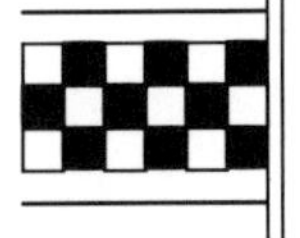

Barbecued Spareribs

From Morrell Park **Serves 6**

The barbecue sauce for this recipe is excellent and just as tasty on chicken or any time a barbecue sauce is called for. It can be made ahead and freezes well for future use. The ribs can be broiled or barbecued as desired.

BARBECUE SAUCE
1/4 cup red wine vinegar
1/2 cup brown sugar
1 6-ounce can tomato paste
1 tablespoon chili powder
1/4 cup Worcestershire sauce
1/4 cup water
1/4 cup minced onion
1 tablespoon lemon juice
1/4 cup orange juice
1 teaspoon dry mustard
2 teaspoons garlic powder
1/2 teaspoon red pepper
1/2 teaspoon chili sauce or Tabasco
1/4 cup soy sauce

4–5 pounds baby back spareribs, cut into 2-rib pieces
1 large onion, diced
1 teaspoon salt

1. In a saucepan, combine all barbecue sauce ingredients and simmer for approximately 1 hour. Set aside.
2. In a large saucepan, place the spareribs, large onion and salt. Cover with water, bring to a boil, then reduce heat and simmer approximately 10–15 minutes, or until tender.
3. Arrange ribs on a rack in a broiler pan and brush generously with sauce. Broil, or barbecue, brushing occasionally with remaining sauce, until ribs are nicely browned, about 10–15 minutes.

Serving suggestion: Serve with rice, French fries or your favorite potato salad recipe.

Serving suggestion: Roast prime rib is excellent served with mashed or baked potatoes and a green vegetable. Instead of pan gravy, prime rib can be served with a dollop of horseradish sauce (page 186).

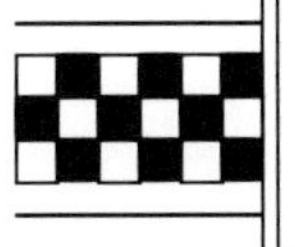

Barbecued Pork Shoulder

From Upton **African American** ***Serves 6***

This is a very tasty traditional Southern pork dish that is sure to bring rave reviews. It can be prepared ahead of time and heated just before serving.

3 1/2–4-pound boneless pork shoulder
Water
1 recipe barbecue sauce (page 88)

1. Preheat oven to 325°.
2. Place pork shoulder in a roasting pan and add water to cover. Bring to a boil on top of stove, cover, then bake in oven for approximately 1 1/2–2 hours, or until very tender. Remove from oven and cool in broth.
3. When cool, cut pork into large cubes.
4. In a large skillet, add pork cubes, cover with barbecue sauce and heat through about 10 minutes, stirring occasionally. Serve.

Serving suggestion: A great dish with collard greens (page 163) and cornbread (page 201).

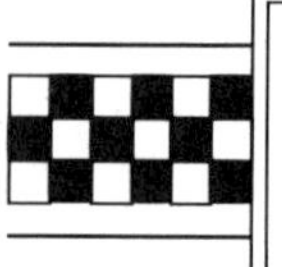

Tonkatsu (Deep-Fried Pork Cutlet)

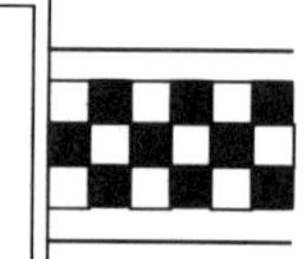

From Charles Center **Japanese** ***Serves 4***

Japanese breadcrumbs, called panko, are used to coat the cutlets. They are not as fine as traditional breadcrumbs and resemble homemade, coarsely crumbled bread.

24 ounces lean, boneless pork loin
2 teaspoons Chinese dried mustard powder*
Salt and pepper to taste
1 cup flour
2 eggs, lightly beaten
2 cups panko* (Japanese-style breadcrumbs)

SAUCE
8 tablespoons tomato ketchup
4 tablespoons Worcestershire sauce
4 teaspoons lemon juice
4 teaspoons prepared mustard
Vegetable oil for deep-frying

1. Slice the pork loin into approximately 8 1/2-inch-thick slices. Pound pork slices until width is reduced by about half.
2. Combine mustard powder with just enough water to form a paste. Spread the paste lightly on each slice of pork and sprinkle with salt and pepper.
3. Dredge the pork slices in flour, dip them in egg and coat with breadcrumbs. Refrigerate for 20 minutes.
4. Meanwhile combine all ingredients for the sauce and mix well. Reserve.
5. Heat oil until hot (about 350°) and fry the cutlets until golden brown, about 5–7 minutes. Serve immediately with the sauce in a separate bowl for dipping.

Serving suggestion: Serve with Chinese vegetables (page 168) or fried eggplant with sweet and sour sauce (page 148).

*Available at Oriental grocery stores.

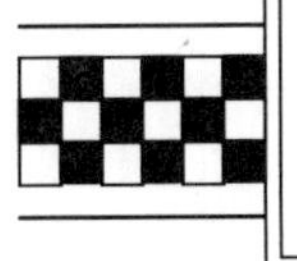

Pork Chop Casserole

From Canton **Serves 4**

This delightful meat and vegetable casserole is uncomplicated to prepare with results sure to please. The cabbage and bread underfilling is tasty and nourishing and can be used as a regular stuffing for pork or poultry.

4 tablespoons unsalted butter
1/2 of a small head of cabbage, chopped
2 celery stalks, minced
1 small onion, minced
1/4 teaspoon sage
1/4 teaspoon thyme
Salt and pepper to taste
3 cups breadcubes
1 egg, slightly beaten
4 pork chops

1. Preheat oven to 350°.
2. In a skillet, melt butter and sauté chopped cabbage 5–10 minutes. Add celery, onion, sage, thyme, salt and pepper and continue cooking another 10–15 minutes. Remove from heat and cool slightly.
3. Place the breadcubes in a bowl. Add the cabbage mixture and the beaten egg and toss.
4. Spread the mixture evenly in the bottom of a casserole. Place the pork chops on top and season with salt and pepper. Bake for approximately 45–60 minutes, or until chops are cooked.

Serving suggestion: Serve with baked sweet potatoes or potato pancakes (page 144).

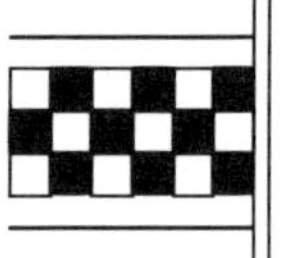

Galareta
Jellied Pigs Feet

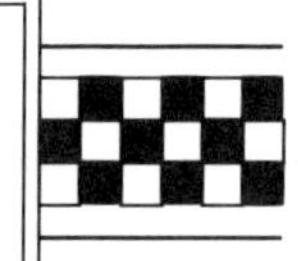

From Fells Point **Polish** ***Serves 4–6***

The stock from cooked pigs feet is very gelatinous and sets firmly when chilled. This dish can be served as part of a buffet and in Poland is served with chilled vodka.

4 pigs feet, halved
2 ham hocks
1 onion, quartered
1 tablespoon vegetable oil
2 celery stalks, chopped
1 sprig parsley
Salt
1 garlic clove
5 whole black peppercorns
5 whole allspice
4 bay leaves
1 tablespoon red wine vinegar
Lemon slices (garnish)
1 hard boiled egg, sliced (garnish)

1. Rinse pigs feet and ham hocks. Place in a large stockpot and cover with water. Bring to a boil, skim off foam that rises to the surface. Lower heat and simmer.
2. Meanwhile, brown onion in oil. Add to stockpot along with celery, parsley, salt, garlic clove, black peppercorns, allspice and bay leaves. Simmer covered for approximately 4 hours or until meat falls off bone easily. Cool in liquid.
3. Strain liquid into a bowl and reserve. Remove meat pieces from strainer and pull off any remaining meat left on bones and add to broth together with the vinegar. Pour just enough broth and meat mixture to fill a loaf pan. Refrigerate until firm, about 6–8 hours or overnight. Scrape off any fat that has risen to the top. Unmold and garnish with lemon slices and hard boiled egg. Slice and serve.

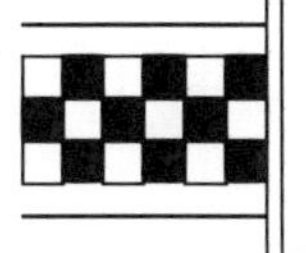

Roast Stuffed Quail

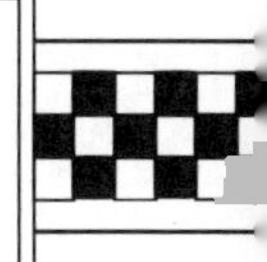

From South Baltimore ***Serves 6***

This dish makes a very elegant presentation for a special dinner party. Quail are more readily available today and can be ordered quite easily. Because they are small in size, two per person should be served.

12 quail
1 medium onion, minced
5 celery stalks, minced
4 tablespoons butter or margarine
Salt and freshly ground pepper to taste
1 teaspoon poultry seasoning
2 tablespoons chopped parsley
4 cups breadcubes
Milk to moisten breadcubes
2 eggs
1 pound white button mushrooms, cleaned and stem tips trimmed
1 cup chicken broth

1. Wash quail and pat dry inside and out. Set aside.
2. In a skillet, sauté onion and celery in butter or margarine until soft. Season with salt, pepper, poultry seasoning and parsley. Reserve.
3. In a large bowl, put the breadcubes and pour in just enough milk to soften. Add the onion mixture and eggs and mix thoroughly.
4. Preheat oven to 400°.
5. Stuff quail with dressing, leaving enough room to place 1 mushroom in each quail. Tie legs together with string.
6. In a roasting pan, place the quail in a circle, leaving the center open. Put remaining stuffing in center, slice remaining mushrooms and place on top of stuffing. Pour chicken broth in pan and roast for about 35–45

minutes, or until the juices run clear when quail is pierced with a fork in the upper thigh. Serve at once.

Serving suggestion: Serve with squash pancakes (page 150) or baked winter squash (page 149).

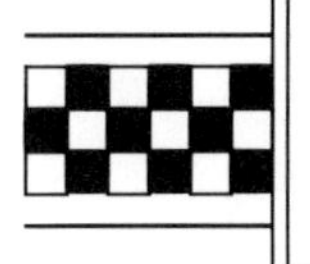

Rabbit Stew

From South Baltimore ***Serves 4***

This recipe originally called for squirrel. Since this is not readily available, rabbit is an excellent substitute. If there are any leftovers, remove meat from bones, heat in remaining sauce and serve over pasta.

2 2 1/2–3-pound rabbits, cut into serving pieces
1 cup flour
1 teaspoon salt
1/2 teaspoon black pepper
1 tablespoon fresh chopped parsley
Oil for frying
2 onions, quartered
3 carrots, cut into 1/2-inch slices
2 potatoes, peeled and quartered
1 teaspoon thyme
1 teaspoon rosemary
1 teaspoon fennel seeds
Zest of 1 orange
3 cups dry red wine
2 cups crushed Italian plum tomatoes

1. In a plastic bag or on a plate, mix together flour, salt, pepper and parsley. Dredge rabbit pieces.
2. Preheat oven to 350°.
3. In a skillet, heat oil and brown rabbit a few pieces at a time. Remove with slotted spoon and place in a roasting pan or Dutch oven. Place onions, carrots and potatoes over rabbit. Sprinkle with herbs and add orange zest and bay leaves. Pour in red wine and tomatoes. Cover and bake for 1 1/2–2 hours, or until rabbit is fork-tender.

Serving suggestion: Serve with rice pilaf (page 181).

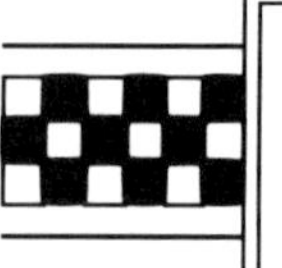

Oxtail Stew

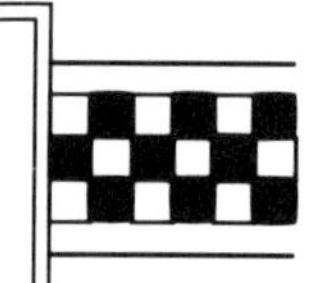

From Roland Park **Serves 4**

A hearty stew for a cold winter's evening. Oxtails are an inexpensive cut of meat best used in soups and stews. They require long cooking that results in tender, succulent meat and a wonderful flavored gravy.

3–3 1/2 pounds oxtails
Flour for dredging
1/4 cup vegetable oil
8 pearl onions
2 celery stalks, cut into 1-inch pieces
4 carrots, cut into 1-inch pieces
2 potatoes, peeled and quartered
4 garlic cloves, minced
1/2 cup dry white wine or dry vermouth
2 tablespoons freshly chopped parsley
1/2 teaspoon marjoram
1/2 teaspoon thyme
1 bay leaf
1 28-ounce can Italian plum tomatoes, with about 1 cup of juice from can
2 1/2 cups beef broth
1 3-inch strip of orange zest
1/3 cup freshly squeezed orange juice
Water
Salt and freshly ground pepper to taste

1. Dredge oxtail pieces in flour.
2. In a Dutch oven or oven-proof casserole, heat oil until hot and brown oxtails on all sides. Transfer to a plate and set aside.
3. Preheat oven to 350°.
4. To the Dutch oven, add the onion, celery, carrots, potatoes and garlic. Reduce heat to medium low and sauté, stirring occasionally for about 5 minutes, or until onions are nicely browned. Add wine and cook 1–2 minutes. Add parsley, marjoram, thyme and bay leaf. Return oxtails to Dutch oven, add plum tomatoes and

juice and, with the side of a spatula, break the tomatoes into pieces. Then add the zest, orange juice and beef broth with just enough water to almost cover oxtails. Add salt and pepper to taste. Cover and bake 3–3 1/2 hours, or until oxtails are very tender.

Serving suggestion: Serve with crusty Italian bread (page 200).

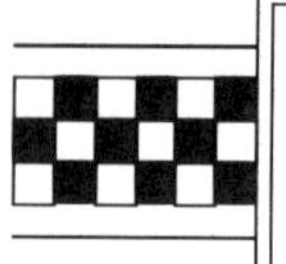

Maryland Kidney Stew

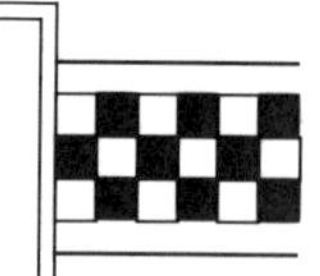

From Lexington Market **Serves 4**

When making this dish use only lamb or veal kidneys. The slow cooking process helps to tenderize the kidneys and makes a delicious, creamy sauce. Traditionally this dish was served for breakfast but is now considered a dinner entree.

4 tablespoons butter
1 small onion, chopped
3 tablespoons flour
2 1/2 cups chicken stock or water
6 lamb kidneys, split, skin and cores removed and thinly sliced
Salt and pepper to taste

1. Preheat oven to 300°.
2. In an oven-proof skillet, melt butter, add onions and sauté until slightly softened. Stirring constantly, mix in flour and cook 1 minute. Gradually add stock or water, stirring to prevent lumps. Add kidneys, salt and pepper and stir to mix.
3. Place in oven and cook for about 4 hours.

Serving suggestion: A great accompaniment to pancakes or biscuits. It can also be served with rice.

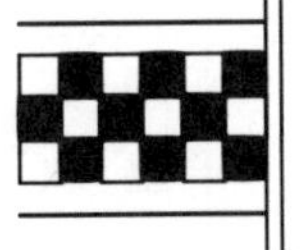

Sautéed Lamb Kidneys

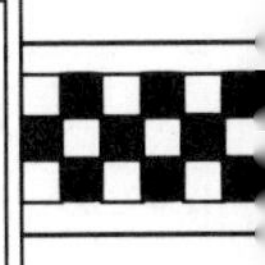

From Morrell Park **Serves 4**

If using beef kidneys, soak in water for 1 hour for a milder flavor. In this recipe be sure to cook kidneys briefly, otherwise they will toughen.

6 lamb kidneys, split, skin and cores removed and thinly sliced
3 tablespoons butter
1/8 teaspoon thyme
1 garlic clove, minced
1/4 teaspoon Worcestershire sauce
Salt and pepper to taste
1/4 cup white wine or water

1. In a skillet, melt butter. Add kidneys and seasonings and cook 1 minute.
2. Pour in wine or water and continue cooking, stirring for another 2–3 minutes. Serve at once.

Serving suggestions: Serve with plain white rice or for breakfast with hot cakes and eggs.

Variation: Substitute veal kidneys for lamb and proceed accordingly.

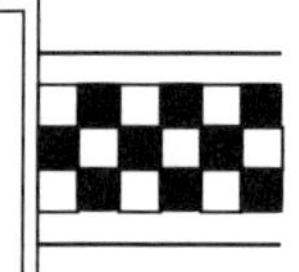

Buffalo Chili

From Lexington Market **_Serves 6_**

If you can find buffalo meat it is a good alternative to beef as it is lower in fat. It also makes an especially tasty chili. This dish also freezes well.

2 tablespoons vegetable oil
1 pound ground buffalo meat
1 onion, coarsely chopped
1 garlic clove, minced
1 19-ounce can kidney beans
4 cups tomato sauce (page 189)
1 tablespoon cornstarch
1 tablespoon chili powder
1 teaspoon paprika
2 teaspoons sugar
Salt to taste

1. In a skillet, heat oil and brown buffalo meat. Add onions and garlic and simmer until onions are soft. Add kidney beans and tomato sauce and simmer 10 minutes.
2. In a small bowl, dissolve cornstarch with about 2 tablespoons of sauce from skillet. Stir back into skillet. Mix in remaining ingredients, cover and simmer about 1 hour, stirring occasionally.

Serving suggestion: Excellent atop noodles or rice or with dumplings (page 146).

Variation: Use lean ground turkey as a substitute for buffalo meat.

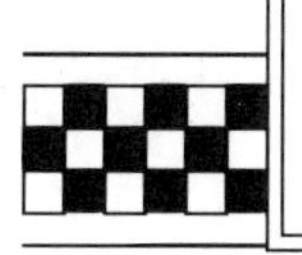

Chorizo (Spicy Sausage)

From Broadway Market, Fells Point **Portuguese** ***Serves 4–6***

Chorizo is a spicy Portuguese sausage. In this recipe you can alter the spiciness by adjusting the amounts of paprika, chili powder and cayenne pepper. These sausages can be served for breakfast or as suggested below.

1 1/2 pounds pork, medium ground
2 teaspoons coarse salt
1/4 teaspoon black pepper
2 tablespoons paprika
1/4 teaspoon oregano
1/4 teaspoon chili powder
1/4 teaspoon cayenne pepper
1/2 cup finely chopped onions
1/2 cup finely chopped green bell peppers
3 tablespoons red wine
Casings for stuffing (optional)

1. In a large bowl, mix all ingredients together and refrigerate overnight.
2. Form mixture into patties and sauté in a small amount of butter or oil for about 4–5 minutes on each side. Serve.
3. If casings are used, rinse them thoroughly in cold water. Using a sausage stuffer or a pastry bag fitted with a wide pastry tip, fill with sausage mixture and insert into opening of casing. Gently squeeze to fill, leaving 4 to 5 inches of casing unfilled at one end. At 4–5-inch intervals, twist casing securely to form links. Break off 2–3 links at a time. In a large skillet, add 1–2 inches of water, bring to boil and add sausages. Reduce heat to medium and cook, turning sausages 2–3 times for about 15–20 minutes, or until cooked through. More water may be needed during cooking.

After the sausages are ready and the water has evaporated, continue cooking, turning often until browned. Serve.

Serving suggestion: Serve with mashed potatoes and a green vegetable.

Variation: Prepare tomato sauce (page 189) and add sausage. Serve with rice.

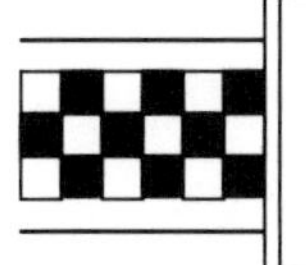

Dolmathakia me Avgolemono

(Stuffed Grapevine Leaves with Egg/Lemon Sauce)

From Locust Point **Greek** ***Makes 42***

The ancient Greeks associated the aroma of mint with strength. Before going into battle, Greek warriors would rub their bodies with the pungent leaves. If fresh grapevine leaves are used, they should be rinsed and blanched in boiling water for 3–4 minutes, then placed in cold water, and drained or patted dry before filling.

1 8-ounce jar preserved grapeleaves*
1 pound ground beef (or 1/2 pound ground beef and 1/2 pound ground lamb)
1 egg
1 medium onion, minced
1/2 cup uncooked rice
1 tablespoon tomato ketchup
2–3 tablespoons chopped fresh (or 1 tablespoon dried) mint
Salt and pepper to taste
3 celery stalks, cut into 1-inch lengths

EGG/LEMON SAUCE
1 egg
Juice or 1 1/2 lemons
1/4 cup reserved cooking juice
Salt and pepper to taste

1. Cover grapeleaves in cold water and soak for 15–20 minutes. Rinse, drain and pat dry. Trim any stems off leaves.
2. In a bowl, combine ground beef with egg. Add milk, onion, rice, ketchup, mint, salt and pepper. Mix thoroughly.
3. To shape rolls, put a leaf, dull side up, on a work surface and place a heaping teaspoon of filling near stem end. Fold sides in and roll up. Proceed filling remain-

ing leaves. Add 1 cup water to bowl in which filling was prepared and reserve.

4. Put celery in bottom of a large, heavy saucepan and place rolls in layers close together, seam side down. Put a plate on top to keep rolls in shape during cooking.

5. Pour water from bowl into saucepan, cover and bring to a boil, reduce heat and simmer about 45 minutes or until rice is cooked. Remove from heat and pour out 1/4 cup liquid from pan. Leave rolls in pan 10–15 minutes, then remove to serving platter while still warm.

6. Prepare egg/lemon sauce. In a small saucepan, beat egg until light and fluffy. Add lemon juice and continue beating. Place saucepan over very low heat and, beating continuously, gradually add in reserved cooking liquid. Continue stirring sauce until thickened, about 3 minutes. Do not bring to boil, or eggs will curdle.

7. Pour sauce over grapeleaves and serve.

*Available in Greek food specialty shops.

Union Square

Union Square is the neighborhood where the sage of Baltimore, internationally famous journalist H.L. Mencken, lived in a 19th-century row house on Hollins Street. The house has been restored and contains many of his belongings and some original furnishings. Another historic site is the Peale Museum, which houses a collection of Baltimore photographs, prints, and paintings.

Fish and Shellfish

Little Italy

Little Italy is tucked between Fells Point and Inner Harbor. It is a neighborhood of small streets with blocks and blocks of row houses, popular family owned and operated restaurants, and bakeries full of delicious breads and pastries. It is a wonderful place to dine and stroll.

Maryland Crab Cakes I

From Union Square ***Makes 6 crab cakes***

Crab cakes are a Maryland tradition. They can be assembled ahead and frozen. To cook, defrost completely in refrigerator before frying.

- 1 egg, beaten
- 4 tablespoons mayonnaise
- 1/3 cup breadcrumbs
- 1 tablespoon minced fresh parsley
- 2 teaspoons Worcestershire sauce
- 1 teaspoon prepared mustard
- Salt and freshly ground pepper to taste
- 1 pound lump crabmeat, picked through to remove cartilage
- Breadcrumbs for coating crab cakes
- 1/4 cup vegetable shortening for frying
- 1 lemon, cut into wedges (garnish)

1. In a bowl, combine beaten egg, mayonnaise, breadcrumbs, parsley, Worcestershire sauce, mustard, salt and pepper and mix well.
2. Pour mixture over crabmeat and toss gently but thoroughly.
3. Form into 6 crab cakes and coat with breadcrumbs. Refrigerate 15 minutes.
4. Heat shortening in a skillet until hot but not smoking. Fry crab cakes until golden on one side, then turn and cook other side. Drain on paper towels. Serve at once with lemon wedges.

Serving suggestion: Serve with French fries and coleslaw.

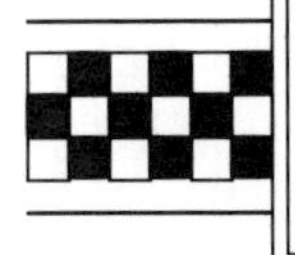

Maryland Crab Cakes II

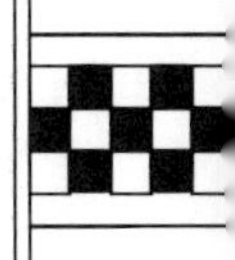

From Govans ***Makes 6 crab cakes***

This is a slightly more substantial version of traditional crab cakes. These cakes can also be baked or broiled instead of frying.

1 pound crabmeat, picked through to remove cartilage
2 slices bread, crust removed and crumbled
1 teaspoon baking powder
1 tablespoon chopped parsley
1 teaspoon Old Bay seasoning
2 teaspoons dry mustard
1 egg white, beaten
3 tablespoons mayonnaise
Breadcrumbs for coating crab cakes

1. Preheat oven to 425°.
2. In a bowl, add crabmeat and fold in the remaining ingredients. Form mixture into 6 cakes. Lightly coat with breadcrumbs.
3. Place on a baking sheet and bake for 8 minutes on each side, or until lightly golden. (Crab cakes may also be broiled, approximately 5 minutes on each side.)

Serving suggestion: Serve with mixed green salad with anchovy dressing (page 187).

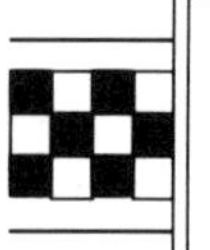

Balmer's Best Crab Cakes

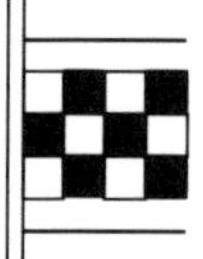

From Little Flower, Belair Edison

Makes 6 crab cakes

This old family recipe for crab cakes uses beaten egg whites, which give the cakes their light texture.

2 egg whites
2 slices dry white bread, crust removed and crumbled
1 tablespoon mayonnaise
1 teaspoon prepared mustard
1/2–3/4 teaspoon Old Bay seasoning
1 pound lump crabmeat, picked through for cartilage
Vegetable oil for deep-frying
Cocktail sauce (page 185) or tartar sauce (page 190)

1. In a bowl, beat egg whites until stiff. Add bread, mayonnaise, mustard and Old Bay seasoning and toss thoroughly but gently.
2. Spoon mixture over crabmeat and gently mix together.
3. Form mixture into 6 large or 8 medium crab balls and chill approximately 1 hour.
4. Heat oil until hot but not smoking and deep-fry crab balls until golden, about 5–10 minutes. Drain on paper towels. Serve at once.

Serving suggestions: Serve with French fries and cole-slaw, or with squash pancakes (page 150) or potato pancakes (page 144).

Fried Stuffed Hard Crabs

From Lexington Market ***Serves 4***

This is a Baltimore favorite. Once the stuffing is eaten, as with most steamed crab recipes, a wooden mallet and fingers are essential to really enjoy the succulent meat.

4 Maryland hard crabs, steamed (page 113)
1 recipe Maryland Crab Cakes (page 109)

BATTER
3 cups pancake mix
2 teaspoons Old Bay seasoning
1–2 cups milk
Oil for deep-frying

1. Remove apron and top shell of crab. Take out fat and gills.
2. Fill cavity of crab with crab cake mixture and press firmly into place. Repeat with remaining crabs.
3. To make batter, combine the dry ingredients in a bowl. Gradually add enough milk to form a fairly thick batter.
4. In a deep-fryer or large saucepan, heat oil until hot.
5. Meanwhile dip each crab into the batter and coat completely, allowing excess batter to drain off.
6. Deep-fry stuffed crabs until well browned on all sides, about 4–5 minutes. Drain on paper towels and serve at once.

Serving suggestions: Serve with coleslaw or a tossed green salad.

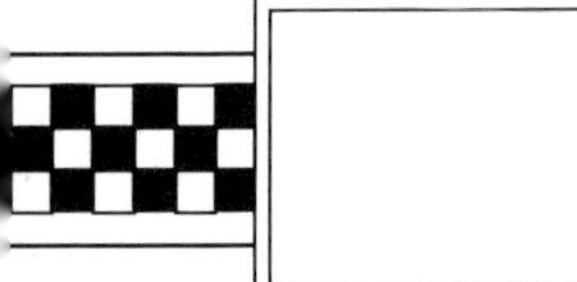

Steamed Blue Crabs

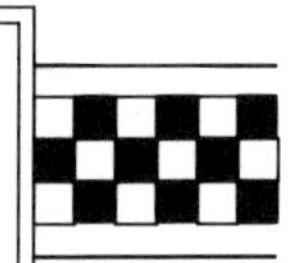

From Lexington Market **Serves 6**

There are three types of hard crabs—blue, Dungeness and king crabs. The Atlantic and Gulf coasts are known specifically for blue crabs. When buying crabs, choose the liveliest in the barrel.

1 cup white wine
Water
1 1/2 dozen live crabs
1/4 cup Old Bay seasoning

1. In a steamer or large stockpot with rack, pour in wine and enough water to come up just below steamer rack.
2. Place 6–8 crabs on rack and sprinkle with Old Bay seasoning. Cover tightly and steam until crabs turn bright red in color, about 20–25 minutes. Remove crabs from steamer and cook remaining crabs. (The quantity of crabs cooked at one time depends on the size of your steamer. Crabs should not be several layers high when cooking.)
3. To serve, place crabs on newspaper-covered table and with wooden mallets and fingers, crack shells and pick clean.

Serving suggestion: Excellent with ice-cold beer.

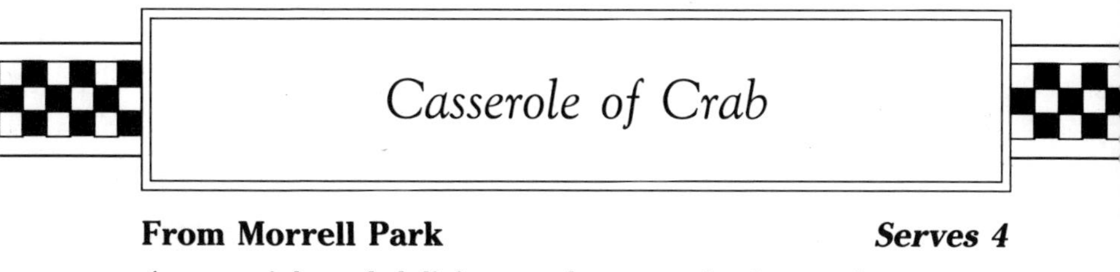

Casserole of Crab

From Morrell Park ***Serves 4***

A very rich and delicious crab casserole that makes a great party dish.

4 tablespoons unsalted butter
4 tablespoons flour
1 teaspoon dry mustard
1 teaspoon cayenne pepper
1 teaspoon garlic salt
1 small onion, chopped
1 cup milk
1 cup half-and-half
1 tablespoon Worcestershire sauce
1 tablespoon lemon juice
1/4 cup red wine
1 cup mayonnaise
2 pounds lump or backfin crabmeat, picked through to remove cartilage
2 cups shredded Cheddar cheese

1. Preheat oven to 350°.
2. In a large saucepan, melt butter, add flour and mix. Stir in mustard, cayenne pepper, garlic salt and onion. Remove from heat.
3. Pour milk and half-and-half into the flour mixture. Return to stove and whisk over low heat until smooth. Add worcestershire sauce, lemon juice, red wine and mayonnaise and stir thoroughly until slightly thickened. Remove from heat.
4. In an au gratin dish or casserole, alternate layers of crab, sauce and cheese, ending with a layer of cheese, and bake for 30 minutes. Serve at once.

Serving suggestions: Serve with rice pilaf (page 181) or plain noodles.

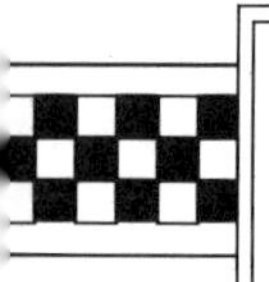

Baked Crab Imperial

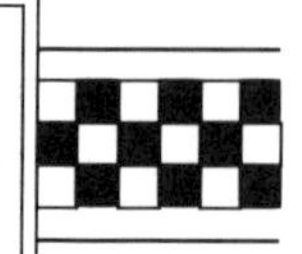

From Hollins Market, Sowebo ***Serves 4***

This recipe can also be used for making crab cakes. The addition of green peppers and celery gives a new twist to a favorite traditional casserole.

1 pound lump crabmeat, picked through for cartilage
1 egg, beaten
1 teaspoon Worcestershire sauce
1 small onion, minced
1 green pepper, minced
1 celery stalk, finely diced
1 tablespoon chopped parsley
1/2 teaspoon dry mustard
1 tablespoon mayonnaise

1. Preheat oven to 350°.
2. In a bowl, combine all ingredients together. Place in an au gratin dish or shallow casserole and bake for 15–20 minutes. Serve.

Serving suggestion: Serve with plain rice and a green vegetable.

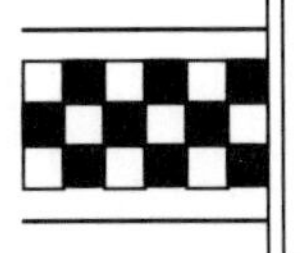

Lobster and Crab Benjamin

From Lexington Market ***Serves 4***

Although there are many ingredients in this dish, it is quite straightforward and well worth the effort. The presentation is attractive and your guests will appreciate the wonderful flavors in this dish. If lobster base is unavailable, 2 tablespoons of clam juice may be used. Also keep in mind that any leftovers make a wonderful sauce for pasta.

2 1/2–3-pound cooked lobster
1 stick unsalted butter
1/2 cup dry white wine
1 teaspoon chopped fresh parsley
1 red bell pepper, diced
1/2 green bell pepper, diced
3 scallions, chopped
1 shallot, chopped
6 mushrooms, chopped
1/2 teaspoon Old Bay seasoning
1/2 teaspoon dried basil
Juice from 1/2 lemon
1/2 teaspoon white pepper

SAUCE
1 cup heavy cream
1 teaspoon lobster base
2 tablespoons dry sherry
1 teaspoon tomato paste
1 tablespoon butter
1 tablespoon flour
Dash of nutmeg
Dash of Old Bay seasoning
1 pound lump crabmeat, picked through for cartilage

1. With a large knife, cut lobster from head to tail until almost through the shell. Remove meat from tail and set aside. Pull out vein, sac and spongy tissue and discard. On underside of claws, cut with scissors to remove the meat without breaking claws and set aside.
2. In a skillet, melt butter and add all ingredients apart from those for the sauce and crabmeat. Sauté gently until vegetables are tender, about 10 minutes. Set aside and let cool to room temperature.

3. To make sauce, place cream, lobster base, dry sherry and tomato paste in a 2-quart saucepan. Whisk over low heat until smooth.
4. Mix butter and flour together to make a paste and blend slowly into sauce, whisking until smooth. Do not boil. Add nutmeg and Old Bay seasoning and stir to mix.
5. Cut lobster meat into bite-size pieces and mix with crabmeat. Incorporate into vegetable mixture.
6. Preheat oven to 350°.
7. Place lobster flat in a baking pan with claws extended. Open shell and fill with crab and lobster mixture. Spoon sauce over mixture. Bake for 15 minutes, then broil to lightly brown for 1–2 minutes. Serve immediately.

Serving suggestion: Serve with rice pilaf (page 181) and salad.

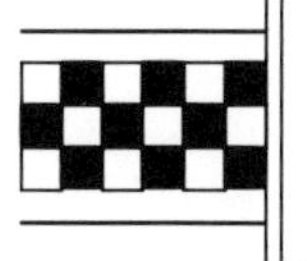

Deviled Lobster Tails

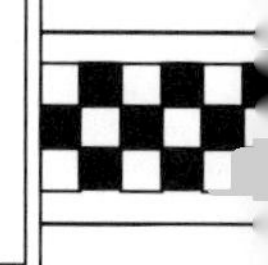

From Morrell Park **Serves 4**

If using frozen lobster tails, make sure to defrost in the refrigerator thoroughly before steaming. This very tasty topping would go equally well with other shellfish.

8 6–8-ounce lobster tails

TOPPING

1 large onion, minced
1 teaspoon Season All
1/8 teaspoon paprika
2 teaspoons lemon juice
1/2 teaspoon dry mustard
1/3 cup breadcrumbs
1/4 cup mayonnaise
2 tablespoons butter, melted
1 teaspoon garlic salt
1/2 teaspoon Worcestershire sauce
1/4 teaspoon Tabasco sauce

1. In a steamer or stockpot, steam lobster tails for about 10 minutes, or until red in color. Cool, remove meat carefully from lobster tails and put back into shell.
2. To make topping, combine all ingredients in a bowl and mix well.
3. Place stuffed lobster shells on a baking tray, spread topping over each lobster and broil 4–5 minutes, or until golden brown. (Do not broil too close to flame.) Serve.

Serving suggestion: Serve with linguine with oil and garlic (page 173) and a green salad.

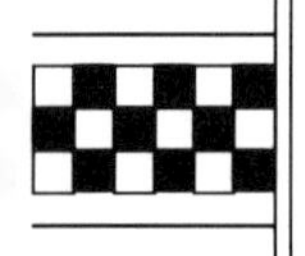

Shrimp with Tofu

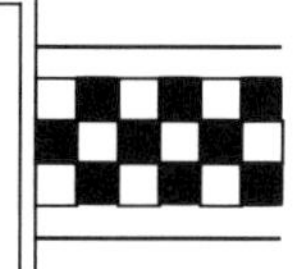

From Charles Village **Chinese** ***Serves 4***

Dried shrimp is often used in Oriental cooking. It has a very strong, intense aroma, but when rehydrated becomes less pungent. The combination of shrimp and tofu gives a wonderful taste and texture to this dish.

1 cup dried shrimp*
1/4 cup peanut oil
2 pieces tofu,* cut into 1/2-inch cubes (about 1 cup)
3 tablespoons soy sauce
Water
1/2 teaspoon spicy chili oil* (optional)

1. In a bowl, place dried shrimp, cover with hot water and let stand for 1 hour. Drain and reserve liquid.
2. In a skillet or wok, heat oil until hot. Stir-fry the tofu until it turns a light golden color, about 1–2 minutes. Add shrimp and 2 tablespoons of the reserved liquid. Mix quickly, then add the soy sauce and about 2–3 tablespoons water and stir-fry for 2–3 minutes longer. At this point, add the chili oil if you prefer a spicy flavor.

Serving suggestion: Serve with steamed rice and stir-fried bok choy (page 164).

Variation: Use thinly sliced pork instead of shrimp and rice wine vinegar instead of the reserved shrimp liquid.

*Available at Oriental food stores.

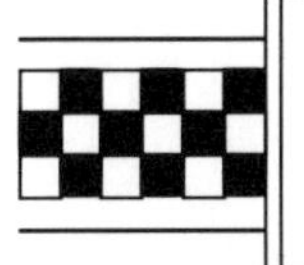

Bobo de Camarao (Baked Shrimp with Coconut Sauce)

From Charles Center **Brazilian** ***Serves 4***

Manioc root is also known as cassava and yuca. It has a brownish skin, which resembles an elongated potato and should always be peeled before cooking. Tapioca is processed from the cassava root, and the so-called pearl tapioca must be soaked before using. Because manioc root and tapioca are starchy, they are mainly used as thickeners in soups and stews throughout Latin America.

1 pound medium shrimp, peeled and deveined
2 tablespoons lemon juice
1/4 cup chopped parsley
1 bay leaf
1 onion, chopped
1 cup cooked manioc root or 1/2 cup tapioca soaked in water 1–2 hours
1/4 cup vegetable oil
4 tomatoes, peeled, seeded and chopped
1 cup unsweetened coconut milk
Salt and pepper to taste
1/2 tablespoon hot pepper sauce

1. In a large glass baking dish, combine shrimp, lemon juice, parsley, bay leaf and onion and marinate 30–40 minutes.
2. To cook manioc root, peel and cut into chunks. Place in a saucepan of boiling water and cook until soft, about 15 minutes. Drain, mash coarsely with a fork and reserve.
3. Preheat oven to 350°.
4. Drizzle 2 tablespoons of the oil over the shrimp and add tomatoes. Cover and bake 5 minutes. (Shrimp is baked along with marinade.)
5. Meanwhile place cooked manioc or drained tapioca with coconut milk in a blender or food processor.

Purée until smooth. Remove shrimp from oven and pour coconut milk mixture over shrimp. Season with salt and pepper and pour remaining 2 tablespoons oil and hot pepper sauce over shrimp.

6. Return to oven and bake another 5–10 minutes. Serve.

Serving suggestion: Serve with white rice and a salad.

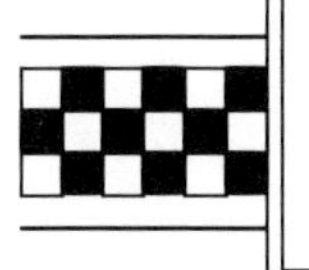

Spicy Shrimp

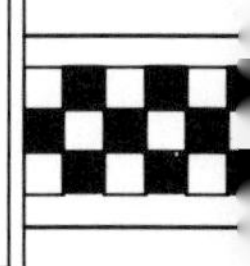

From Little Flower, Belair Edison ***Serves 4***

This is a quick, easy and very tasty shrimp dinner. For the sauce, ketchup may be used instead of the chili sauce, and the seasonings can be adjusted to make it as hot or spicy as you wish.

SAUCE
1 cup chili sauce
1 teaspoon horseradish
1 teaspoon Old Bay seasoning
2–3 dashes hot sauce
1 teaspoon lemon juice

1/2 cup white vinegar
1/2 cup water
1 teaspoon Old Bay seasoning
1 pound shrimp, unpeeled

1. To make sauce, thoroughly combine all ingredients in a bowl and refrigerate until ready to serve.
2. In a saucepan, combine vinegar, water and Old Bay. Bring to a boil, reduce heat, add shrimp and simmer covered for approximately 7–10 minutes. Remove shrimp and serve with spicy sauce.

Serving suggestions: This dish can be served as an appetizer or as an entree along with plain rice.

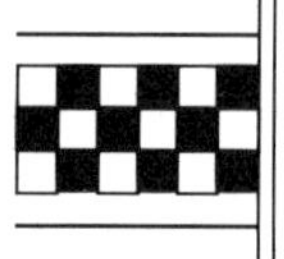

Shrimp Fried Rice

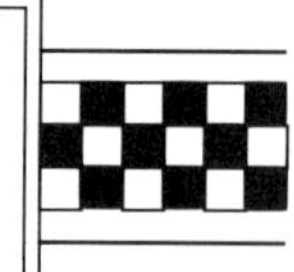

From Waverly **Chinese** ***Serves 4***

The toasted sesame seeds add a nutty flavor to this excellent version of shrimp fried rice.

3 tablespoons peanut oil
3 scallions, chopped
1/2 cup diced red or green bell pepper
1/2 pound small shrimp, cooked, peeled and deveined
4 cups cooked white or brown rice
1 egg, beaten
1 teaspoon sesame seeds, toasted
1 teaspoon sesame oil*

1. In a wok or skillet, heat oil and stir-fry scallions and peppers until tender, about 2 minutes. Add shrimp and rice and stir-fry until just heated through. Pour in beaten egg and with a fork, mix into rice.
2. Remove from heat, sprinkle with sesame seeds and drizzle with sesame oil.

*Available at Oriental and specialty food stores.

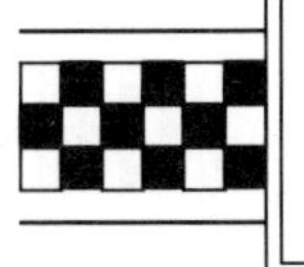

Shrimp "Aiaello"

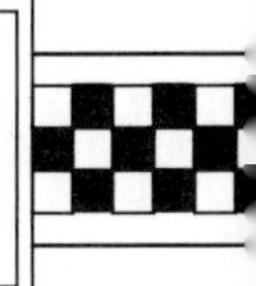

From Mt. Vernon ***Serves 4***

This is a delicious shrimp dish which you will want to prepare time and time again. For this recipe, use whole-milk mozzarella instead of the part skim.

1 1/2 pounds jumbo shrimp, shelled, deveined and butterflied
Old Bay seasoning to taste
1 cup shredded whole milk mozzarella
2 cups tomato sauce (for homemade, see page 189)

1. Flatten shrimp as you place them in one layer in a large, shallow oven-proof casserole. Sprinkle with Old Bay seasoning and cover with mozzarella.
2. Place under the broiler for approximately 8–10 minutes, or until the cheese has melted and the shrimp are cooked.
3. In a saucepan, heat the tomato sauce and pour over and around the shrimp. Serve.

Serving suggestion: Serve with plain rice or pasta and a green salad.

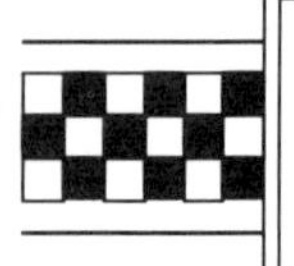

Fried Oysters

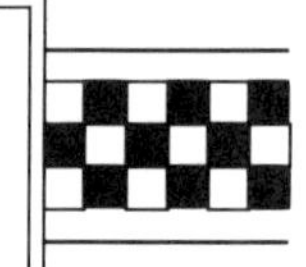

From Northwest Baltimore ***Serves 4***

A helpful hint when preparing shucked oysters: Place them in a sieve or colander over a bowl and refrigerate for 2–3 hours so that they will be well drained before breading and frying.

1 1/2 cups Italian flavored breadcrumbs
1/2 teaspoon paprika
1/2 teaspoon celery salt
1/2 teaspoon garlic powder
2 dozen shucked oysters, well drained
2 eggs beaten with 1 tablespoon water
Vegetable oil for frying
Recipe cocktail sauce (page 185)

1. On a plate, combine breadcrumbs, paprika, celery salt and garlic powder.
2. Dip each oyster in the egg, then coat well with breadcrumb mixture.
3. In a medium saucepan, add oil about 2 inches deep. When oil is hot, fry oysters a few at a time for 2–3 minutes, turning them in the oil until golden on both sides. Do not overcook. Drain on paper towels and serve at once with cocktail sauce.

Serving suggestion: Serve with your favorite coleslaw recipe.

Variation: Place oysters on top of a fresh spinach salad with anchovy dressing (page 187).

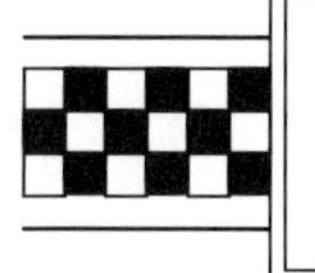

Oyster and Ham Casserole

From Canton ***Serves 4***

This recipe can also be made without a pie crust. Just place oyster mixture in a casserole and bake as described below.

1 pint shucked oysters
2 tablespoons unsalted butter
2 tablespoons flour
1/2 cup chicken stock
1/2 cup milk
1 cup cooked peas
1 cup diced cooked ham
Pinch of black pepper
1 recipe pie crust (page 217), prebaked

1. Preheat oven to 425°.
2. Drain oysters and reserve juice.
3. In a saucepan, melt butter, stir in flour and cook 1–2 minutes. Add 2 tablespoons oyster juice and mix well. Over low heat, gradually pour in chicken stock and milk. Cook, stirring constantly, until thickened, about 5 minutes. Add the reserved oysters, peas and ham, sprinkle with pepper and mix gently.
4. Pour oyster mixture into the prebaked pie shell and bake approximately 15 minutes.

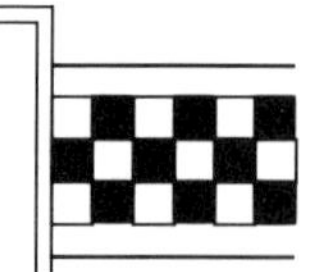

Marinated Broiled Scallops

From Charles Village **_Serves 4_**

During the summer these scallops are great for barbecuing on the outdoor grill. They can also be marinated overnight in the refrigerator and removed 20 minutes before cooking time.

2 1/2 pounds sea scallops
1 teaspoon lemon pepper
5 tablespoons olive oil
3 tablespoons chopped fresh (or 1 1/2 tablespoons dried) rosemary
1/8 teaspoon dried red pepper flakes

1. In a bowl, place the scallops and sprinkle with lemon pepper.
2. In another bowl, mix remaining ingredients. Pour mixture over the scallops and toss. Cover bowl with plastic wrap and allow to marinate at room temperature for about 1 hour.
3. Heat broiler and place scallops on a broiling pan (scallops may also be skewered). Broil for 2–3 minutes, turn and broil for another 2–3 minutes. Do not overcook. Serve at once.

Serving suggestion: Serve with linguine with oil and garlic (page 173) and crusty Italian bread (page 200).

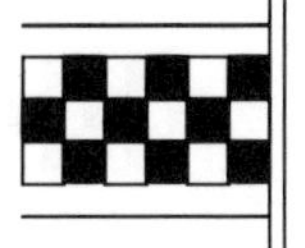

Seafood Norfolk

From Govans ***Serves 4***

Old Bay seasoning is a combination of many spices, including pepper, laurel, cloves, ginger, mace, cardamom and paprika. It enhances many seafood dishes. When in season oysters may also be added to this casserole.

1 pound shrimp, shelled and deveined
1 pound sea scallops
1/4 pound cooked lobster meat
1/4 pound crabmeat, picked through for cartilage
1/4 cup Parmesan cheese
1 tablespoon lemon juice
1 teaspoon Old Bay seasoning
1/2 teaspoon onion powder
1/2 teaspoon garlic powder
1/2 teaspoon white pepper
1/4 cup breadcrumbs
1/4 cup chopped pimentos
1 cup dry white wine

1. Preheat oven to 350°.
2. Place the shrimp, scallops, lobster and crabmeat in an au gratin or baking dish.
3. Combine remaining ingredients, except for the wine, and toss with the seafood. Pour white wine over mixture and bake for approximately 15–20 minutes, or until seafood is just done. Serve at once.

Serving suggestion: Plain rice is a perfect accompaniment for this seafood casserole, along with sautéed zucchini and red peppers (page 151).

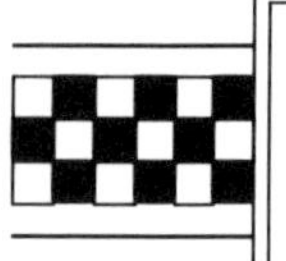

Bacalhau Podre (Codfish Casserole)

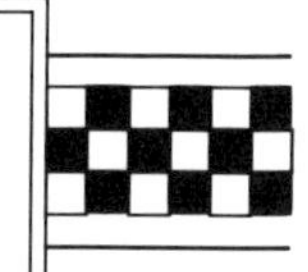

From Highlandtown **Portuguese** ***Serves 4***

Codfish is popular throughout the Mediterranean. This Portuguese casserole is yet another wonderful way of preparing salt cod.

1–1 1/4-pound piece salt cod
1 tablespoon flour
6 eggs
Vegetable oil for frying
2 medium potatoes, peeled and sliced into 1/4-inch rounds
1 large onion, thinly sliced
2 garlic cloves, minced
1/3 cup chopped fresh parsley
Freshly ground pepper to taste
1/2 cup water

---

1. Place cod in a pan, cover with water and soak 2 days in the refrigerator, changing water 4–5 times. Drain and pat dry. Cut into serving-size pieces.
2. In a bowl, place flour and beat in 1 egg until thoroughly mixed.
3. In a skillet, add enough vegetable oil to cover bottom and heat until hot. Dip cod pieces into flour/egg mixture, letting excess egg drip off, add to skillet and fry over medium high heat until golden on both sides. (Fish should be cooked through.) Keep warm.
4. Adding a little more oil to skillet if needed, fry potato slices until cooked. Remove and reserve.
5. In the same skillet, sauté onions and garlic until soft. Mix in parsley and with a slotted spoon remove mixture to a plate. Reserve.
6. In a casserole or Dutch oven, place half the potatoes, top with half the onion mixture and cover with half

the codfish. Add remaining potatoes and codfish and top with remaining onions. Season with freshly ground pepper.

7. Beat together remaining 5 eggs with water and pour into casserole. Place on top of stove and simmer gently until egg has set and fish has heated through.

Serving suggestion: Serve with a tossed green salad and Italian bread (page 200).

Variation: Add sliced green olives and pimentos to the onion mixture. Casserole may also be baked in the oven at 350°.

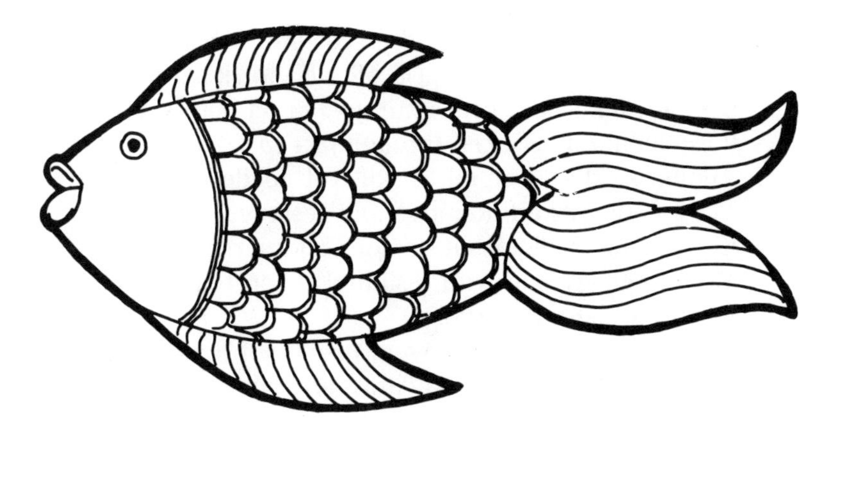

Bacalhau a Sagres com Hortela (Baked Cod)

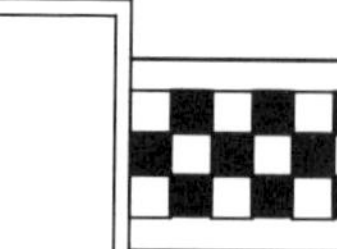

From Highlandtown **Portuguese** ***Serves 4***

Salt cod is featured in many different dishes in Portugal. Use Portuguese beer if it is available; if not, substitute an imported European or Brazilian beer. It is best to use fresh mint for this dish.

- 1 1/2 pounds salt cod
- 3 small onions, sliced
- 2 tomatoes, peeled, seeded and diced
- 2 garlic cloves, minced
- 2 sprigs fresh mint, chopped or 1 teaspoon dry mint
- 1 large red bell pepper, diced
- 1/4 cup olive oil
- 3 potatoes, peeled and sliced
- 1 cup beer

1. Place cod in a pan, cover with water and soak 2 days in the refrigerator, changing the water 4–5 times.
2. Preheat oven to 350°.
3. Drain cod and remove any bones and skin. Cut into 3-inch strips and place in a casserole in one layer.
4. Cover the top of the cod with onions and tomatoes and sprinkle with garlic and mint. Add peppers and drizzle with some of the olive oil.
5. Place the potato slices around the cod. Pour in beer and drizzle with remaining oil. Bake for approximately 45 minutes, or until fish flakes easily with a fork and the potatoes are cooked.

Serving suggestion: Serve with noodles or rice and a green salad.

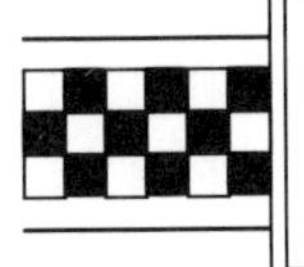

Bacalhau Fritters (Codfish Cakes)

From Highlandtown Portuguese *Makes 12–16 cakes*

The secret to success in making these codfish cakes is the dryness of the mixture; otherwise the cakes may fall apart during frying.

1 pound salt cod, soaked in water overnight
3 potatoes, boiled and well drained
2 tablespoons chopped parsley
1/2 cup grated onion
Freshly ground pepper to taste
1 egg yolk
Vegetable oil for deep-frying

1. Remove cod from water and cook in boiling water for 5 minutes. Remove and drain thoroughly. Shred cod, removing any bones, and place in a large bowl.
2. In another bowl, coarsely mash the well-drained potatoes. Mix into shredded cod thoroughly but gently.
3. Add the parsley, onion, pepper and egg yolk and mix well. (The mixture should be fairly dry.)
4. Scoop up a quantity of the mixture the size of an egg and form into compact oval shapes.
5. In a deep saucepan, add enough oil to come halfway up pan. Heat until hot and fry cod cakes a few at a time until dark golden in color, about 3–5 minutes. Serve hot.

Serving suggestion: Serve with tartar sauce (page 190) and a green salad.

Variation: Any leftovers make an excellent sandwich with sliced tomato and lettuce on crusty Italian bread (page 200) or pita bread.

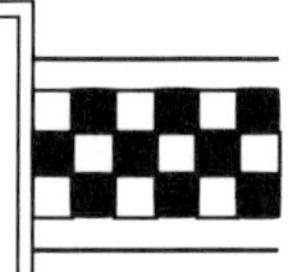

Crab-Stuffed Bluefish

From Mt. Vernon **Serves 4**

The crab complements the richness of the bluefish and makes this an outstanding dish.

- Oil for greasing pan
- 1 cup crabmeat, picked through for cartilage
- 1/2 teaspoon Worcestershire sauce
- 1/2 teaspoon Old Bay seasoning
- Pinch of salt and pepper
- 2 tablespoons chopped parsley
- 1 egg, beaten (1 tablespoon mayonnaise may be substituted)
- 1 2-pound or 2 smaller whole bluefish, cleaned and boned, with head left on
- Lemon slices (garnish)

1. Preheat oven to 425°.
2. Brush baking pan with oil.
3. In a bowl, combine crabmeat, Worcestershire sauce, Old Bay seasoning, salt, pepper and parsley. Mix well. Fold in gently the beaten egg or mayonnaise.
4. Place the fish on a surface and open. Sprinkle with salt and pepper. Place crab mixture along one side of the fish cavity and close the opening with toothpicks.
5. Lay fish on prepared baking pan and bake for 15–20 minutes, or until fish is cooked and flakes easily with a fork. The skin should be crispy.
6. Place on serving dish, cut into thick slices and garnish with lemon.

Serving suggestion: Serve with red pepper and zucchini sauté (page151).

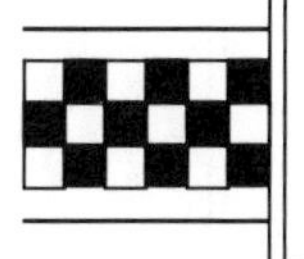

Fish Fry

From South Baltimore ***Serves 4***

The surprise in this recipe is the use of potato buds. They add an extra crispness to this fried fish. Potato buds can be used as a coating for other fried foods as well.

- 1 1/2–2 pounds fish fillets (flounder, bluefish, etc.)
- 2 eggs, beaten with 2 tablespoons water
- 2 cups instant potato buds
- Vegetable oil, for frying

1. Dip fish fillets in eggs, then coat with potato buds.
2. Heat oil in a skillet over medium heat until hot. Fry fish until golden brown on one side, then turn and brown the other side. Fish should flake easily with a fork when cooked. Serve.

Serving suggestions: Serve with kim chee (page 161) or Chinese vegetables (page 168).

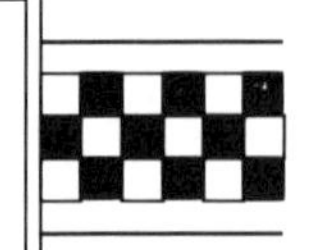

Pan-Fried Lake Trout

From Northwest Baltimore ***Serves 4***

Lake trout are small freshwater fish. For this recipe brook, pan or oyster trout may be used as a substitute.

1 cup flour
1 cup cracker meal
Salt and pepper to taste
4 small lake trout
2 eggs, beaten
Vegetable oil or shortening for frying

1. On a plate, mix the flour, cracker meal, salt and pepper together.
2. Dip the fish into the egg, then coat with the flour mixture.
3. In a skillet, add about 1 inch of oil, heat until hot but not burning and fry the fish until golden, about 4–5 minutes on each side. Serve at once.

Serving suggestions: Serve with coleslaw or hot cabbage salad (page 44).

Variation: Instead of whole fish, fish fillets may be used.

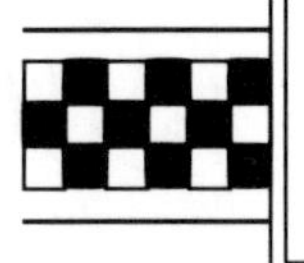

Mediterranean Baked Fish

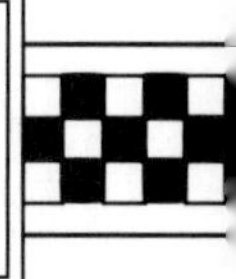

From Edmondson Village **Jewish** ***Serves 4***

To prepare fish for Kosher cooking, the whole fish should be salted and refrigerated overnight, then rinsed thoroughly and patted dry before using.

2 potatoes, sliced 1/4-inch thick
2 tomatoes, sliced 1/4-inch thick
3 garlic cloves, minced
1–1 1/2 pounds fish fillets (scrod, haddock or bluefish)
Salt and freshly ground pepper to taste
1/4 cup chopped fresh parsley
1/4 cup vegetable oil flavored with a pinch of hot red pepper flakes (strain oil before using to remove flakes)
3/4–1 cup water

1. Preheat oven to 350°.
2. In a casserole large enough to hold the fish in a single layer, place sliced potatoes on the bottom. Top with tomatoes and garlic. Place fish on top (fish may be cut into pieces to fit on top of the potatoes and tomatoes). Season with salt and pepper, sprinkle with parsley and drizzle with the flavored oil.
3. Add water to casserole and bake approximately 40–45 minutes, or until fish and potatoes are done.
4. With a spatula, lift a portion of potatoes, tomatoes and fish and place on a plate. Pour a little of the pan juices over the fish. Garnish with additional chopped parsley, if desired, and serve.

Baked Fish

From Belair Market, Old Town ***Serves 4***

A very simple, easy and tasty dish. The fish, wrapped in foil, bakes in its own juices, which keeps it moist during cooking.

2 1 1/2–2-pound fish (sea trout, sea bass), cleaned with head and tail left on

1 package onion soup mix (shake packet well to mix spices)

1. Preheat oven to 350°.
2. Place each fish on a piece of aluminum foil large enough to enclose it.
3. Sprinkle half the onion soup mix on each fish and wrap the foil securely around each one. Place on a baking sheet.
4. Bake approximately 30 minutes, or until fish flakes easily with a fork. Serve the fish with the accumulated juices.

Serving suggestion: Serve with baked potato.

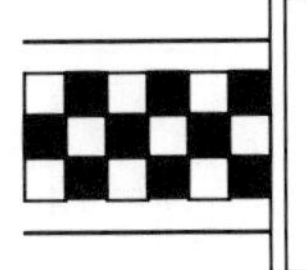

Scapece alla Vastese (Marinated Fried Fish)

From Little Italy **Italian** ***Serves 4***

This can be used as a light, refreshing antipasto or first course as well as an entree. Saffron is used in many Mediterranean and Asian dishes. It has a pungent flavor and should be used sparingly. Store in an air-tight container in a dark place.

1 teaspoon saffron
2 cups white wine vinegar
1/4 cup olive oil
4 fish fillets (flounder, fluke, whiting or eel), cut into serving pieces
Flour for dredging
Salt to taste

1. In a saucepan, dissolve saffron in 3 tablespoons of vinegar. Let stand 3 minutes and pour in remaining vinegar. Reserve.
2. In a large skillet, heat oil. Dredge fish with flour and fry until brown on both sides. Carefully lift fish from skillet and drain on paper towels. Sprinkle with salt. Place in a shallow dish large enough to accommodate the fish in one layer.
3. Bring reserved vinegar to a boil and pour over fish. Allow to marinate in refrigerator overnight. Bring to room temperature before serving. Drain fish in vinegar, bring to room temperature. Serve.

Serving suggestion: Serve with rice pilaf (page 181).

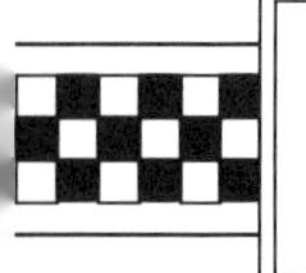

Ryba w Galarecie (Fish in Aspic)

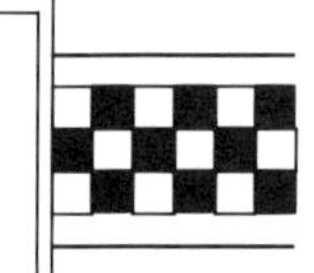

From Howard Park **Polish** ***Serves 4***

Aspic should preferably be made from a good, strong, flavorful homemade broth. For a quick aspic, use bottled clam juice and simmer with fish bones and vegetables for about 20 minutes.

6 cups water
2 carrots, cut into chunks
1 celery stalk, cut into chunks
1 onion, halved
2–3 sprigs fresh parsley
4 black peppercorns
1 3-pound whole whitefish (sea trout, pike or carp), cleaned, with head removed (reserve head for stock)
1 egg white
1 tablespoon gelatin and 2 tablespoons water for aspic
12 capers (garnish)

1. In a large saucepan, add the water, carrots, celery, onion, and parsley. Bring to a boil and simmer 1 hour. Add peppercorns and fish head and simmer an additional 40 minutes. Strain the stock. (You may need to add more water or white wine to make a total of 5 cups of stock, if too much liquid has evaporated.)
2. Preheat the oven to 350°.
3. Place the fish in a baking dish and pour on the reserved stock. Bake for 15–20 minutes, or until the fish flakes easily with a fork. Carefully remove fish and place on a large platter.
4. Strain the liquid from the baking dish to remove any fish particles and put into a large saucepan. To clarify the stock, beat the egg white lightly and add to the stock. Heat gently and simmer for 10 minutes. Do not allow it to boil. Remove from heat and let stand for 10

minutes. The egg whites collect the impurities and will rise to the surface. Remove them with a skimmer. Strain the stock through a sieve lined with a wet cheesecloth to remove any further impurities.

5. Dissolve the gelatin in water and add to the stock, beating thoroughly to dissolve. Let thicken slightly. Gently spoon mixture over fish until completely covered and chill overnight.
6. To serve, garnish with capers.

Serving suggestion: Serve with a cucumber and tomato salad.

Vegetables

Patterson Park

Patterson Park now lies on the site of Hapstead Hill. Baltimore's first park contains cannon that saw use during the War of 1812 and an octagonal observatory known as the "Chinese Pagoda," which allows a fine view of the harbor and downtown Baltimore.

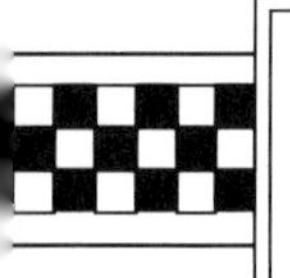

Au Gratin Potatoes

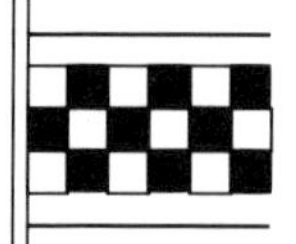

From Mount Vernon ***Serves 4***

A delicious, creamy potato casserole topped with a luscious layer of cheese that goes so well with many dishes.

Butter for greasing

2 baking potatoes, peeled and thinly sliced
1/2 cup chicken stock
1/2 cup heavy cream or half-and-half
Salt and freshly ground pepper to taste
2 tablespoons unsalted butter
1/2 cup grated Gruyere cheese (Swiss, Cheddar, Parmesan or a mixture of these cheeses may be used.)

1. Preheat oven to 350°.
2. Butter the bottom and sides of an 8-inch casserole. Add the sliced potatoes and pour in stock and cream. Season with salt and pepper and dot with butter.
3. Sprinkle cheese over top of potatoes and bake for approximately 1 hour, or until potatoes are cooked and cheese has browned. Serve.

Serving suggestions: Serve with roast prime rib of beef (page 47), rolled stuffed pork roast (page 84) or stuffed veal roast (page 63).

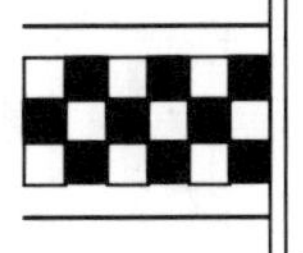

Potato Pancakes

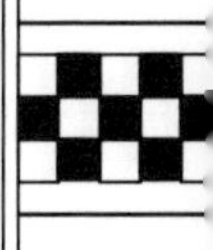

From Hollins Market, Sowebo **German** ***Serves 4***

Potatoes are a wonderful accompaniment to many dishes. This is a very easy and delicious way of preparing potatoes and is traditionally served with apple sauce or sour cream.

5 potatoes, peeled and grated
2 eggs, beaten
Salt and pepper to taste
Pinch of nutmeg
1 cup flour
1 small onion, grated (optional)
vegetable oil for frying

1. In a bowl, mix together all the ingredients.
2. In a skillet, add enough oil to coat the bottom. Heat oil until hot. Scoop about 2 tablespoons of mixture and drop into hot oil. Flatten slightly and brown on both sides, about 1–2 minutes. Several pancakes can be cooked at the same time, but do not overcrowd skillet.
3. Drain and serve at once.

Serving suggestions: Serve with pork chop casserole (page 92) or roast stuffed chicken (page 68).

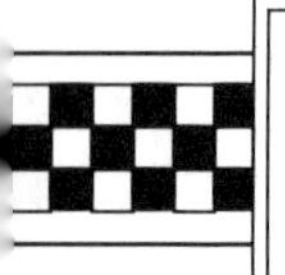

Sweet Potato Pudding

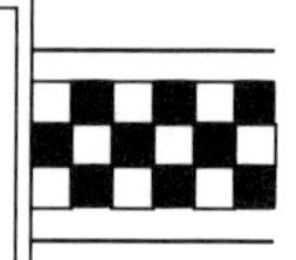

From Irvington **African American** ***Serves 6–8***

This is a very rich version of sweet potato pie. It resembles a bread pudding and is sometimes served as a dessert. Sweet potatoes or yams should be stored in a cool, dark place to prevent quick spoilage.

Butter for greasing
3 medium sweet potatoes, boiled, peeled and mashed
3 eggs
1/2 stick margarine, melted
1/2 cup granulated sugar
1/2 cup self-rising flour
1 tablespoon vanilla
1/4 teaspoon ground cinnamon
1/4 teaspoon ground nutmeg
1/2 cup raisins
1/2 cup milk
1/2 cup crushed black walnuts (optional)

---

1. Preheat oven to 350°.
2. Butter a 7 1/2-inch round soufflé dish.
3. In a bowl, combine all ingredients with mashed potatoes. Pour into soufflé dish and bake approximately 45–60 minutes, or until top is lightly browned. Cool slightly and serve.

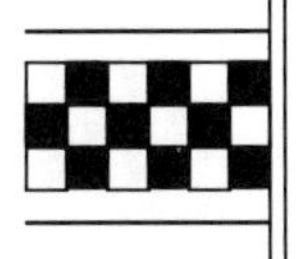

Potato Dumplings

From Patterson Park German *Makes 18 dumplings*

When recipes call for nutmeg, it is best to buy whole and freshly grate it. It has a sweet bouquet and a rich, woody flavor.

2 potatoes, peeled, boiled and mashed (about 2 cups)
1/4 cup farina
1/4 cup all-purpose flour
Salt and freshly ground pepper to taste
Freshly grated nutmeg
1 egg, lightly beaten

1. In a bowl, combine mashed potatoes, farina, flour, salt, several grindings of fresh pepper and a little grated nutmeg. Beat well.
2. Fill a large saucepan with water and bring to a boil. Reduce heat to low.
3. With floured hands, form the mixture into balls (about golf ball size) and drop them one at a time into the simmering water. Cook approximately 10–15 minutes, or until they rise to the top. Remove with a slotted spoon and serve at once.

Serving suggestions: Serve along with sauerbraten (page 49) or red cabbage (page 160).

Variation: Melt 6 tablespoons unsalted butter, add 1 cup breadcrumbs and 1/2 teaspoon dried parsley flakes and cook 1–2 minutes, stirring constantly. Remove from heat and as dumplings are cooked, roll in the buttered breadcrumbs to coat.

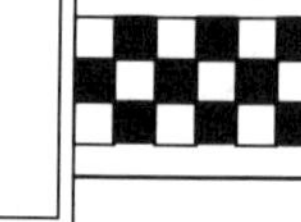

Stuffed Eggplant

From Belair Market, Old Town ***Serves 4***

This dish is excellent made with very small Japanese eggplants. If available, 6–8 of these can be substituted for 4 small regular eggplants.

4 small eggplants, sliced lengthwise
1 tablespoon olive oil
1/2 cup finely diced green bell pepper
1/2 cup minced onion
1/4 teaspoon thyme
1/4 teaspoon oregano
1/2 pound ground beef or ground turkey
1/4 cup tomato sauce
1 tablespoon tomato paste
Salt and pepper to taste

1. Scoop flesh from eggplant halves and dice finely. Place shells in a baking dish.
2. Preheat oven to 350°.
3. In a skillet, heat oil. Add peppers, onions, diced eggplant, thyme and oregano and cook 1–2 minutes. Add ground meat and brown for 5 minutes. Stir in tomato sauce and paste and cook another 10 minutes, or until the liquid has almost evaporated.
4. Fill eggplant shells with mixture. (This can be prepared ahead of time.) Bake for 15–20 minutes. Serve at once or at room temperature.

Variation: Add 2 cups of tomato sauce to baking dish and bake as above.

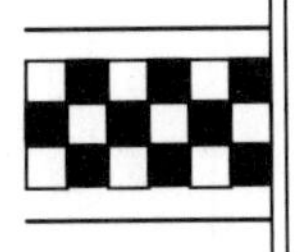

Nasu Kara Age
(Fried Eggplant with Sweet and Sour Sauce)

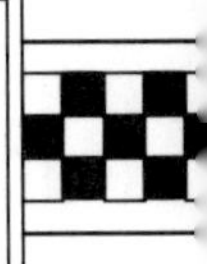

From Cross Street Market, Federal Hill **Japanese** ***Serves 4***

Japanese eggplants are milder and have fewer seeds than the larger variety. When buying, look for eggplants that are firm and have a glossy sheen to the skin.

SWEET AND SOUR SAUCE
1 tablespoon sesame seeds, lightly toasted
2–3 garlic cloves, minced
1 tablespoon red wine vinegar
1 tablespoon sesame oil
2 tablespoons soy sauce
1 teaspoon sugar
1 chili pepper, minced (optional)

Peanut oil for deep-frying
8 small Japanese eggplants or 2 large eggplants, peeled and cut into cubes

1. To make sweet and sour sauce, combine all ingredients in a bowl, mix well and reserve.
2. Heat oil for deep-frying in a saucepan. Fry eggplant until lightly golden and cooked through. Remove and drain well.
3. Arrange eggplant on a platter, pour sauce evenly over top and allow to stand 3–5 minutes before serving.

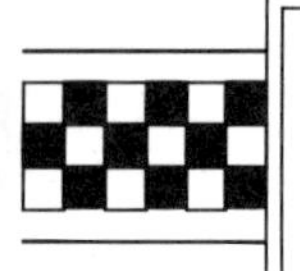

Baked Winter Squash

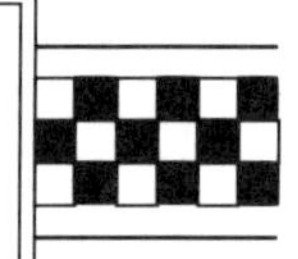

From Cross Street Market, Federal Hill ***Serves 4***

Summer squash, such as zucchini, can be used unpeeled. Winter squash, such as acorn or butternut, have a harder shell and only the inner flesh is eaten.

2 acorn squash, split in half, seeds removed
Water
4 tablespoons butter
Maple syrup for drizzling (optional)

OPTIONAL FILLING
1 apple, peeled and diced
1/2 cup raisins, plumped in warm water to soften

1. Preheat oven to 350°.
2. Place squash, cut side down, in a baking dish. Pour in water halfway up the squash. Bake for about 35–40 minutes, or until almost cooked. Drain liquid from pan, turn squash upright and dot with butter. Drizzle with maple syrup or stuff with the apple/raisin mixture. Continue baking for another 15–20 minutes, or until cooked through.
3. Serve at once.

Serving suggestions: Serve with stuffed veal roast (page 63) or roast fresh pork shoulder (page 86).

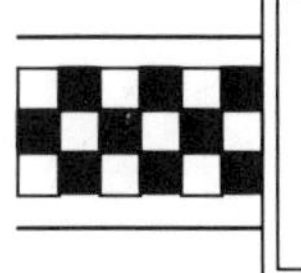

Squash Pancakes

From Belair Market, Old Town/Stirling ***Serves 4***

A nice change from potato pancakes.

3 zucchini (yellow or green), scrubbed clean and grated
1 egg, beaten
1 tablespoon grated onion
1/3 cup flour
Salt and pepper
Oil for frying

1. In a bowl, combine zucchini, egg, onion, flour, salt and pepper. Mix well.
2. In a skillet, add enough oil to coat bottom of pan and heat until hot. Scoop about 2 tablespoons of mixture and drop into hot oil. Fry for 2–3 minutes on each side until crisp. Serve at once.

Serving suggestions: A great accompaniment for meatloaf (page 60), or roast stuffed chicken (page 68).

Red Pepper and Zucchini Sauté

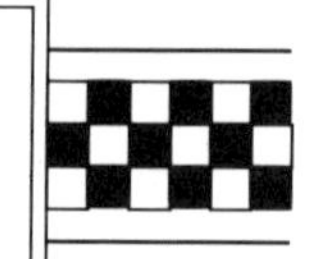

From Guilford **Serves 4**

A quick, delicious, colorful vegetable dish to serve with meat, fowl or fish.

- 2 tablespoons butter
- 2 tablespoons olive oil
- 2 large red bell peppers (or a combination of red and green), cored and sliced into 1/2-inch-thick strips
- 2 medium zucchini, scrubbed, ends trimmed and sliced into 1/4-inch-thick rounds
- Salt and pepper to taste

1. In a skillet, heat butter and oil over medium heat. Add peppers and fry, stirring for 2–3 minutes. Reduce heat and continue cooking until peppers are tender.
2. Add zucchini, stirring often, until cooked. Serve.

Serving suggestions: Serve with grilled veal chop (page 67) or grilled scallops (page 127).

Variation: Add assorted vegetables, such as sliced onions, tomatoes and mushrooms.

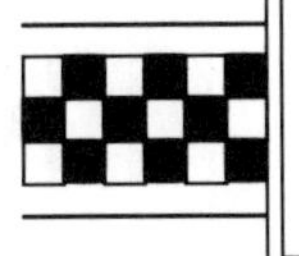

Zucchini in Sour Cream

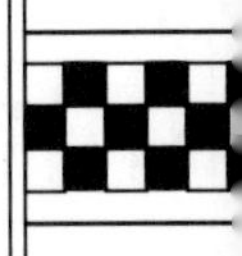

From Broadway Market **Ukrainian** ***Serves 4***

This vegetable dish is a refreshing change from plain boiled or steamed zucchini. The delicate flavor of dill compliments this sauce.

1 pound zucchini, cut in half lengthwise and sliced thinly
Salt
1 tablespoon cornstarch
1 cup sour cream
3 tablespoons butter or margarine
1 onion, chopped
1 garlic clove, minced
Freshly ground pepper to taste
2 tablespoons chopped fresh dill
2 tablespoons white wine vinegar

1. Sprinkle zucchini with salt and let stand 20 minutes.
2. In a small bowl, combine cornstarch and sour cream. Reserve.
3. In a skillet melt butter, add onion and garlic and sauté until softened, about 5 minutes.
4. Drain zucchini and squeeze out excess liquid. Add zucchini to skillet, season with salt and pepper and cook 15 minutes, or until tender.
5. Add reserved sour cream mixture and heat gently, about 2–3 minutes.
6. Stir in dill and vinegar and heat another 1–2 minutes. Serve at once.

Serving suggestions: Rolled stuffed pork roast (page 84) or crab stuffed bluefish (page 133).

Variation: Instead of zucchini, use raw thinly sliced cucumbers.

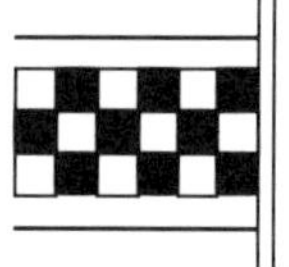

Stuffed Peppers

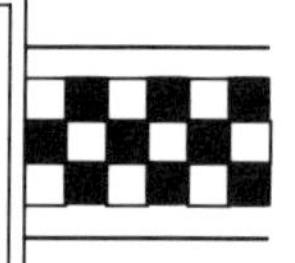

From Broadway Market, Fells Point ***Serves 4***

For a colorful presentation, use a combination of red, yellow and green peppers. Any leftover stuffing may be used to make stuffed mushrooms.

4 bell peppers, seeded and cored
1 tablespoon butter
1 small onion, minced
1/2 stalk celery, minced
1 garlic clove, minced
1/4 pound ground beef
4 tablespoons soy sauce
1/8 teaspoon white pepper
1/2 cup uncooked white rice
1/2 cup uncooked wild rice
1 1/2 cups water
Oil for greasing pan and for drizzling over peppers

1. In a large saucepan, bring water to a boil, add peppers and blanch for 3–4 minutes. Remove and drain.
2. In a skillet, melt butter and sauté onions, celery and garlic until soft. Add ground beef and brown about 3–4 minutes. Stir in soy sauce and pepper. Add white and wild rice to skillet. Pour in water, lower heat and simmer until rice is cooked and water absorbed, about 25 minutes.
3. Preheat oven to 350°.
4. Oil a baking pan large enough to hold peppers.
5. Stuff peppers with filling and place standing upright in baking pan. Drizzle remaining oil over peppers and bake for 25–30 minutes, or until tender. Serve hot or at room temperature.

Serving suggestion: Serve with a good, crusty Italian bread (page 200).

Variation: Add 2 cups crushed tomatoes to pan and bake as above.

Corn Pudding

From Cherry Hill **Serve 4**

This traditional corn pudding has a light, soufflé-like texture. In the summer, use fresh corn instead of canned.

2 eggs
1 cup milk
Pinch of sugar
Pinch of salt
1 tablespoon cornstarch or flour
1 small onion, diced
1 8 1/2-ounce can creamed corn
1 7-ounce can whole-kernel corn
Butter for greasing

1. Preheat oven to 350°.
2. In a bowl, mix eggs, milk, sugar and salt. Whisk in cornstarch until smooth. Add onion and cans of corn and mix thoroughly.
3. Butter a 7×7-inch casserole. Pour in corn mixture and bake 45 minutes, or until puffed and golden on top. Serve at once.

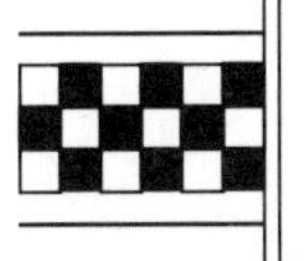

Palak Paneer (Spinach with Cheese)

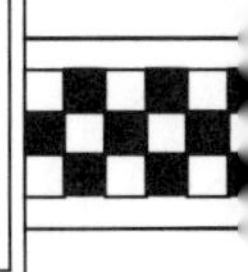

From Charles Center **Indian** ***Serves 4***

Paneer is an Indian curd cheese which you can very easily make at home. Tofu may be substituted because it has a similar consistency and taste, but the dish would be less authentic.

PANEER
8 cups whole milk (not skimmed or low-fat milk)
4 tablespoons lemon juice
Vegetable oil for frying

SPINACH MIXTURE
2 tablespoons vegetable oil
1 large onion, chopped
1 large tomato, diced
1 1/4 teaspoons garlic, minced
1/4 teaspoon fresh ginger, minced
1/4 teaspoon salt
1/2 teaspoon chili powder
1/2 teaspoon cumin powder
1/2 teaspoon coriander powder
2 bunches spinach, washed and coarsely chopped

1. To make paneer, add milk to a large saucepan. Gradually bring to a boil, stirring occasionally to prevent a skin from forming on top. When milk has reached boiling point, lower heat and pour in lemon juice. With a spoon or fork, stir the milk gently in a figure-eight pattern. (Do not scrape against the bottom or sides of saucepan.) After a few seconds, curds will start to form. Continue stirring gently for 2–3 minutes.
2. Line a strainer with cheesecloth and place over a large bowl. Gently pour curdled milk into strainer. The liquid (whey) will drain through, leaving the curds behind. Drain thoroughly. Gently gather cheesecloth together and squeeze out any remaining liquid. (It's important

that curds be very dry.) Wrap cheesecloth completely over curds, put back in strainer and place a heavy weight on top. Refrigerate for 2–3 hours, or until curds are firm to the touch.

3. Remove from refrigerator and cut cheese into cubes. In a non-stick skillet, add enough oil to come halfway up side of pan. Gently fry cheese until light golden on all sides. Place in a bowl of ice water and refrigerate until needed.

4. To assemble, heat vegetable oil in a skillet. Add onions and cook until lightly browned. Add tomatoes and spices and cook for 10 minutes over low heat.

5. Stir in spinach and simmer for a further 10 minutes. With a slotted spoon, remove cheese from water and add to spinach. Heat through 5 minutes. Serve.

Serving suggestion: Serve with chicken tikka masala (page 76).

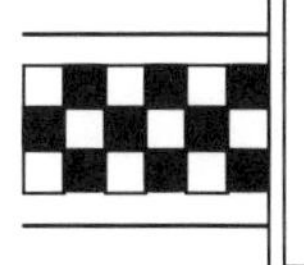

Spanakopita (Spinach and Cheese Pie)

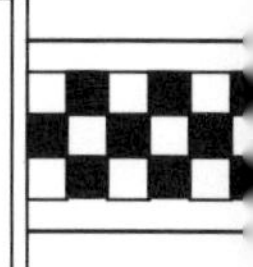

From Fells Point **Greek** ***Serves 8–10***

Feta is a cheese made from goat's milk. It is lower in fat than some other cheeses. To store, place in brine or milk, changing liquid every few days. Feta is a versatile cheese and is delicious crumbled or sliced over a green tossed salad.

1/2 pound (2 sticks) unsalted butter or margarine
1 medium onion, minced
3 10-ounce packages frozen chopped spinach, thawed and well drained
4 large eggs
1/2 pound feta
1/4 cup chopped parsley
2 tablespoons chopped dill
Salt and pepper to taste
16 phyllo leaves, room temperature

1. Preheat oven to 350°.
2. In a medium-sized skillet, melt 4 tablespoons of the butter and sauté onion until lightly golden, about 5 minutes. Stir in spinach, remove from heat and set aside.
3. In a large bowl, beat eggs well and stir in cheese, parsley, dill, salt and pepper. Add spinach and onion mixture and mix well.
4. In a small saucepan, melt remaining butter. Brush a 13×9×2-inch baking pan lightly with some of the melted butter and place 1 sheet of phyllo on bottom. Brush sheet with a little butter and continue layering with 7 more sheets, buttering each sheet.
5. Spread spinach mixture evenly over phyllo and continue layering and buttering with the remaining 8 sheets. Brush top sheet of phyllo with butter and, using scissors, trim edges of phyllo.

6. Place in oven and bake 30–35 minutes, or until top is puffed and lightly golden. Remove from oven and allow to cool slightly before cutting into squares.

Serving suggestions: Serve with Greek meatballs (page 62) or roast chicken with herb bread stuffing (page 68).

Variation: Instead of a regular onion, use several chopped scallions. Cottage and cream cheese may also be added to spinach mixture.

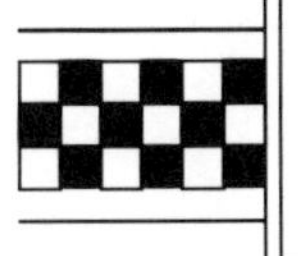

Braised Red Cabbage

From Patterson Park **Polish** ***Serves 4***

Red cabbage is a lovely fall vegetable that goes well with most game dishes. It tastes even better a day or two later, either heated through or at room temperature.

1/4 pound thickly sliced bacon, diced
1 onion, chopped
1 head red cabbage, shredded
2 Granny Smith apples, peeled, cored and sliced
1/4 cup red wine vinegar
1/4 cup dry red wine
1/2 teaspoon caraway seeds
6 juniper berries, crushed
Salt to taste

1. In a saucepan, fry bacon and onion until onion has softened. Stir in remaining ingredients except salt, cover with lid slightly askew and simmer, stirring occasionally, for 30–40 minutes, or until cabbage is cooked. Add salt to taste.
2. Serve hot or cold.

Serving suggestions: A good accompaniment to stuffed quail (page 94) or sauerbraten (page 49).

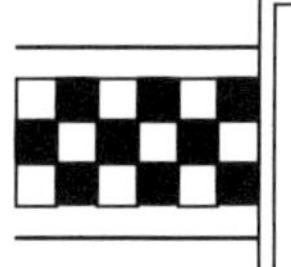

Kim Chee (Pickled Cabbage)

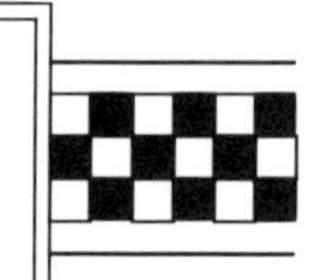

From Lafayette Market **Korean** ***Makes 4–6 cups***

During the marinating process, kim chee takes on an acidic taste, which mellows with time. It can be kept refrigerated for about 2 weeks.

- 1 large head Chinese cabbage
- 3 tablespoons salt
- 4 scallions, cut into 1 1/2-inch lengths, then cut into thin slices (use top green part also)
- 1 large garlic clove, minced
- 1 tablespoon hot red pepper flakes
- 1 teaspoon grated ginger root

1. Cut cabbage into 1×1-inch pieces and place in a bowl. Sprinkle with 2 tablespoons salt, mix well and let stand for 15 minutes. Rinse and drain.
2. Add scallions, garlic, pepper flakes, ginger root, the remaining 1 tablespoon of salt and enough water to cover the ingredients. Cover and let stand at room temperature for 2 days. Refrigerate for another 2 days. With a slotted spoon, remove cabbage and serve.

Serving suggestions: An excellent accompaniment for deep-fried pork cutlets (page 91), barbecued beef (page 59) or stir-fried flank steak (page 56).

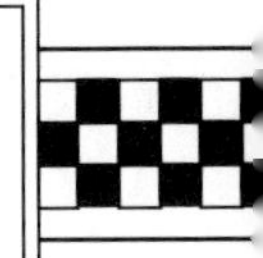

Stuffed Cabbage

From Locust Point ***Serves 6–8***

This is an especially good vegetable entree to serve with mashed potatoes because of the wonderful tomato gravy.

1 head cabbage
1 pound ground round
1/2 pound ground pork
1/2 pound ground veal
1/3 cup uncooked rice
1 onion, minced
1 egg
Salt and pepper to taste
2 10 3/4-ounce cans tomato soup
2 tablespoons butter

1. With a sharp knife, remove the core from cabbage.
2. In a large stockpot, cover cabbage with water, bring to a boil and cook for approximately 20 minutes. Remove leaves as they start to soften. Place in colander to drain. When cabbage is cool enough to handle, separate leaves gently and trim down any thick stems on each leaf.
3. In a bowl, mix together ground round, pork, veal, rice, onion, egg, salt and pepper.
4. Preheat oven to 350°.
5. Take a heaping tablespoon of meat mixture and place in center of cabbage leaf. Fold sides in and roll. Continue filling remaining leaves.
6. In a large roasting pan, place rolled cabbage in rows close together, making two layers. Pour in tomato soup along with 1 can of water, dot with butter, cover and cook for approximately 1 1/2 hours.

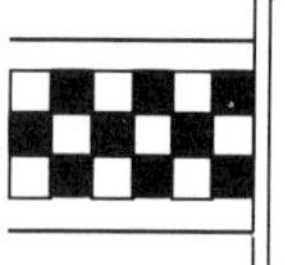

Collard Greens

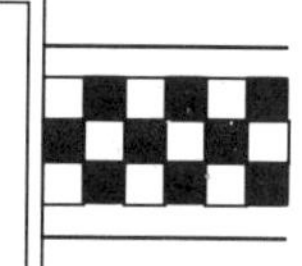

From Upton **African American** ***Serves 4***

Collard greens are available year round and are a very popular vegetable. They are usually prepared with salt pork, ham hock or bacon.

2–3 bunches collard greens
1 pound salt pork, diced or 1 thick-sliced piece of bacon, diced
1 onion, chopped
1/4 teaspoon marjoram
Water

1. Cut stems from greens and wash thoroughly in several changes of water. Drain.
2. In a large saucepan over low heat, cook salt pork or bacon until golden in color. Add onion, greens and marjoram and cook at a simmer for 25–30 minutes, or until greens are tender. (The greens cook with the water clinging to the leaves after rinsing. If necessary, add some additional water during cooking to prevent sticking or burning.)
3. Remove greens to a platter and serve.

Serving suggestion: Collard greens may be served with barbecued spareribs (page 88).

Stir-Fried Bok Choy

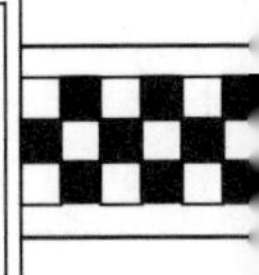

From Cross Street Market, Federal Hill **Chinese** ***Serves 4***

Bok choy is a small, white, stemmed cabbage with green leaves. It has a delicious flavor and should be cooked briefly and served immediately.

2 pounds bok choy
3–4 tablespoons peanut oil
1 teaspoon sugar
1 teaspoon salt
White pepper to taste
1/4 cup dry sherry
3 tablespoons soy sauce
2/3 cup hot water

1. Wash bok choy and slice stems diagonally into 1-inch lengths. Slice the leaves in half.
2. In a skillet, heat oil until hot. Add stems and stir-fry quickly 2 minutes. Add leaves and stir-fry 1 minute. Sprinkle with sugar, salt and white pepper. Stir in sherry, soy sauce and hot water. Reduce heat to low, cover and cook 1 minute longer.
3. Serve at once.

Serving suggestions: Serve with barbecued spareribs (page 88) or roast fresh pork shoulder (page 86).

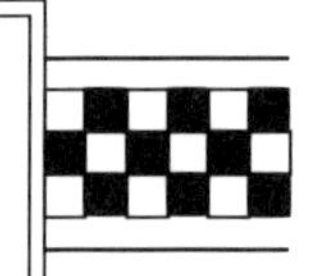

Southern Black-Eyed Peas

From Upton **African American** ***Serves 4***

Soaking peas overnight reduces cooking time.

1 cup dried black-eyed peas picked through to remove any stones or pebbles
Water
1 onion, peeled and quartered
1 stalk celery, coarsely chopped
1 ham hock or several slices thick bacon
Pinch of sugar (optional)

1. Place peas in a bowl of water to cover and soak overnight. Drain.
2. In a large saucepan, add peas, 1 quart water, onion, celery, ham hock and sugar, if desired. Bring to a boil, skim any residue off top, lower heat and simmer for about 2 hours, or until peas are tender. If necessary, add additional water to saucepan. The consistency should be like a very thick stew.

Serving suggestion: Serve with Baltimore fried chicken (page 75) and cornbread (page 201).

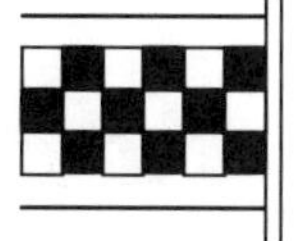

Mushroom Pie

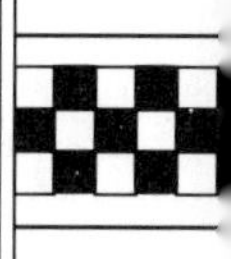

From Southwest Baltimore ***Serves 8***

Mushroom pie can be served for a light luncheon with a mixed green salad. To make this dish even more interesting, use a combination of mushrooms, such as shiitake, chanterelle and oyster.

6 tablespoons butter
2 pounds mushrooms, wiped clean, stem tips removed, cut into thick slices
Juice from half a lemon
Salt and pepper to taste
6 tablespoons flour
1 cup chicken broth
1/4 cup Madeira
1/2 cup heavy cream
1 recipe pie crust (page 217), uncooked
1 egg, beaten

1. In a large skillet, heat 4 tablespoons of the butter, add mushrooms, and sprinkle with lemon juice, salt and pepper. Cover and cook over medium heat for 10 minutes, shaking pan often.

2. Remove mushrooms with a slotted spoon and arrange in a buttered 9-inch pie plate. To skillet pan juices, stir in remaining 2 tablespoons butter and flour and gradually pour in chicken stock. Cook, stirring, until sauce is thick and smooth, about 10 minutes. Stir in Madeira and heavy cream, season with salt and pepper and pour over mushrooms.

3. Preheat oven to 450°.

4. Roll out pie crust large enough to cover mushroom filling. Brush dough with egg and make a few slits on top to release steam while cooking. Bake 15 minutes, reduce heat to 350° and bake another 10–15 minutes, or until crust is lightly golden.

5. Remove from oven, let sit a few minutes, slice and serve.

Serving suggestions: Serve with roast prime rib of beef (page 47) or Baltimore fried chicken (page 75).

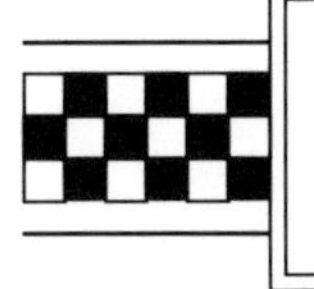

Stir-Fried Mixed Vegetables

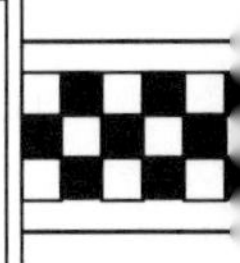

From Cross Street Market, Federal Hill **Chinese** ***Serves 6–8***

Derived from the Chinese words for white and vegetable, bok choy is a wonderful addition to this mixed vegetable stir-fry.

2 quarts water
2 cups broccoli florets
2 cups cauliflower florets
3 stalks bok choy
3 celery stalks
1/4 pound mushrooms, cleaned, stem tip removed and sliced
3 tablespoons peanut oil
2 tablespoons soy sauce
2 tablespoons dry sherry
1 teaspoon sugar
1/2 cup chicken broth
1 tablespoon cornstarch
2 tablespoons cold water

1. In a large stockpot, bring water to a boil and add broccoli and cauliflower. Boil for 1 minute, drain and rinse in cold water. Pat dry.
2. Slice bok choy and celery into 1/4-inch diagonal slices.
3. Heat a skillet over high heat. Add oil and when hot, reduce heat to medium high and add broccoli, cauliflower and celery. Stir-fry 1 minute. Add mushrooms and bok choy and stir-fry 2 minutes. Stir in soy sauce, sherry, sugar and broth until boiling.
4. Mix together cornstarch and 2 tablespoons cold water. Add to skillet and stir constantly until thickened. Serve.

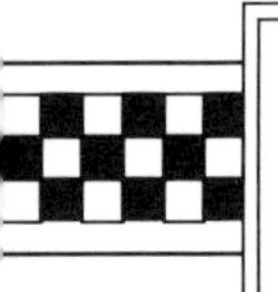

Braised Fennel

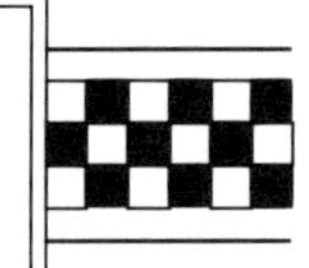

From Northeast Baltimore ***Serves 4***

Fennel has a slight anise taste which, when cooked, brings out its subtle flavor. When used raw in a salad, its taste is more pronounced.

4 medium fennel bulbs, tops trimmed off
2 cups chicken stock
1 tablespoon Parmesan cheese
1 tablespoon butter

1. Slice fennel bulbs lengthwise into 1/4-inch slices.
2. In a sauté pan, add fennel slices in one layer (slices may overlap slightly) and cover with chicken stock. Bring to a boil, lower heat, cover and simmer 10–15 minutes, or until fennel is tender. Do not overcook. Drain off any liquid left in pan. Sprinkle with Parmesan cheese and dot with butter. Cover and allow to sit 2–3 minutes before serving.

Serving suggestions: Serve alongside grilled veal chops (page 67) or meatloaf surprise (page 61).

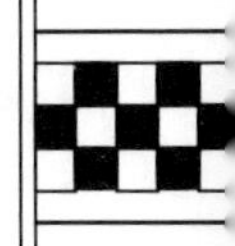

Baked Rutabaga

From Belair Market, Old Town ***Serves 4***

Rutabaga is a winter vegetable with a slight horseradish flavor. It is a nice addition to casseroles and stew or can be puréed and served with game.

3 large rutabagas, peeled, cut in half width-wise and sliced into 1/4-inch-thick pieces
4 tart apples (such as Granny Smith), peeled, cored and thinly sliced
2 tablespoons brown sugar
4 tablespoons butter

1. Preheat oven to 350°.
2. Heat water in a large saucepan and parboil the rutabaga for 5–8 minutes. Drain.
3. In a medium-size casserole, place rutabaga slices in one layer and top with a layer of apples.
4. Sprinkle with sugar and dot with butter. Bake in oven for approximately 30 minutes, or until rutabaga is cooked. (During cooking, 1–2 tablespoons of water may be needed if mixture appears too dry.)

Serving suggestions: Serve with roast fresh pork shoulder (page 86) or rolled stuffed pork roast (page 84).

Pasta and Rice

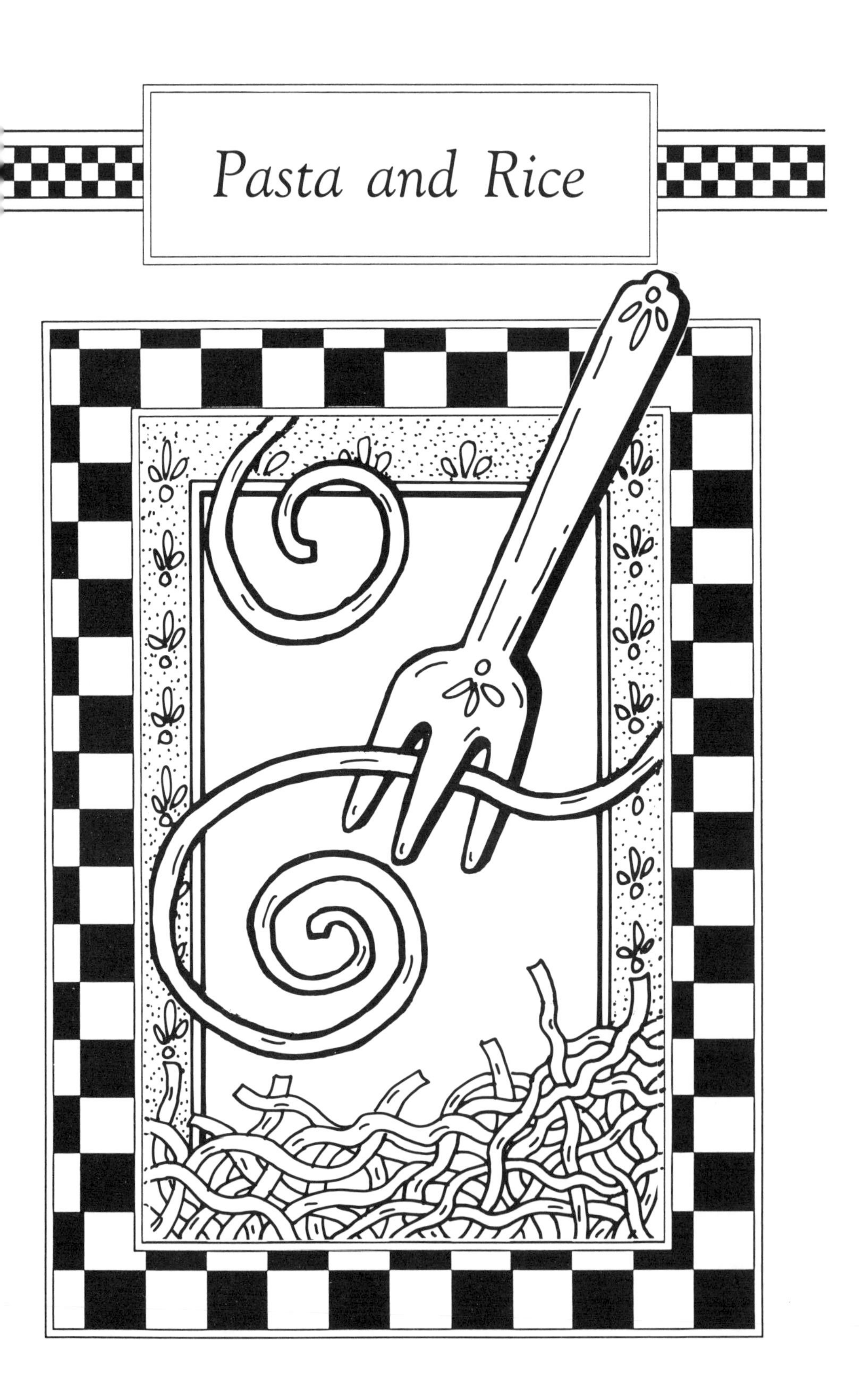

Charles Center

Charles Center is one of the most ambitious urban renewal projects ever undertaken by a major city. It is a mixture of homes, apartments, stores, boutiques, and the first legitimate theater to be built in the United States in many years.

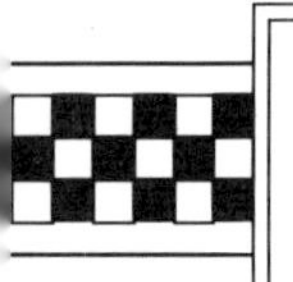

Linguine with Oil and Garlic

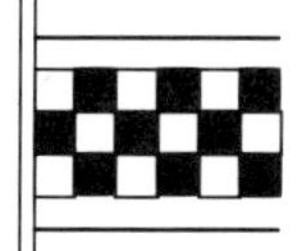

From Little Italy **Italian** ***Serves 4***

In this delicious, easy sauce, use roasted peppers from a jar or rub fresh peppers with oil, arrange on a baking sheet and place in a 300° oven for 15–20 minutes. Peel skin while peppers are still hot.

1 pound linguine
2/3 cup olive oil
4 large garlic cloves, sliced
1/2–3/4 cup green olives, or black olives, pitted and sliced (reserve a few for garnish)
1/2 cup roasted red peppers, sliced
1/2 cup chopped fresh parsley
Salt and pepper to taste

1. Cook linguine until al dente, about 8 minutes. Drain, reserving 2/3 cup of hot water in which pasta was cooked.
2. In a skillet large enough to accommodate the cooked linguine, cover bottom of skillet with olive oil, add garlic and cook over medium heat until lightly golden.
3. Add olives, roasted peppers, parsley, salt and pepper to taste. Cook 1–2 minutes.
4. Thin sauce by adding the reserved 2/3 cup of water. Toss linguine with sauce. Serve at once garnished with additional sliced olives.

Serving suggestions: This dish goes especially well with marinated grilled scallops (page 127) or sautéed veal chop (page 67). It can also be served as an entree with a tossed salad.

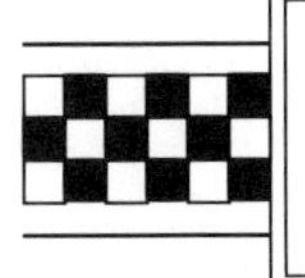

Spaghetti with Pesto

From Little Italy **Italian** ***Serves 4***

Pesto freezes well, but remember not to add Parmesan cheese before freezing. Pesto should be defrosted and cheese stirred in just before serving. Although walnuts may be substituted for pine nuts, they have a stronger, less delicate flavor.

2 cup fresh basil leaves
2 garlic cloves
1/2 cup olive oil
1 tablespoon white wine
3–4 tablespoon pine nuts
1/4 cup Parmesan cheese
1 pound spaghetti or your favorite pasta

1. In a food processor or blender, combine all ingredients except for Parmesan cheese and whiz until smooth or to desired consistency. Mix cheese in thoroughly by hand.
2. Cook spaghetti until al dente, adding 1 or 2 tablespoons of the hot water in which spaghetti was cooked to the pesto sauce to thin slightly. Drain pasta, place in a bowl and toss with the pesto. Serve.

Variation: Pesto can be used as a dressing over sliced tomatoes and mozzarella or stuffed into cherry tomatoes for a quick appetizer.

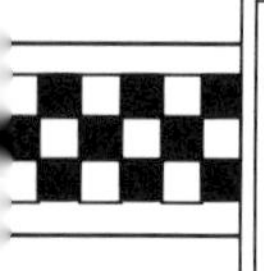

Lasagna

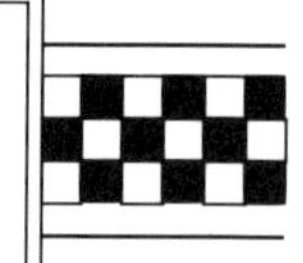

From Little Italy **Italian** ***Serves 6–8***

To prevent lasagna noodles from sticking while cooking, cook a few at a time in boiling water. Drain and sprinkle lightly with oil. The use of lean ground turkey reduces the fat content and results in a lighter yet very flavorful casserole.

1 medium onion, minced
2 tablespoons olive oil
1 large garlic clove, minced
1 pound ground turkey or lean beef
2 15-ounce cans tomato sauce
1 cup water
Pinch of sugar (optional)
1 teaspoon oregano
Salt and pepper to taste
1 pound lasagna noodles
1 15-ounce container ricotta cheese
1/4 cup freshly grated Parmesan
8 ounces mozzarella cheese, grated
2 eggs
Additional Parmesan for sprinkling

---

1. In a large saucepan, sauté onion in oil over a medium low heat until softened. Add garlic and sauté 1–2 minutes longer. Add ground turkey or beef, increase heat to medium high and cook until meat changes color. Add tomato sauce, water, sugar (if used), oregano, salt and pepper and simmer 1 hour. Reserve.
2. Meanwhile cook noodles, a few at a time, until al dente. Drain, separate noodles in a colander or lay on a towel to prevent sticking.
3. In a bowl, combine ricotta, Parmesan, mozzarella and eggs. Season with salt and pepper.
4. Preheat oven to 375°.

5. Spread a little of the meat sauce in a 13×9×2-inch baking pan. Place a layer of lasagna noodles over sauce and top with a little of the cheese filling. Repeat layering with remaining ingredients, ending with a layer of noodles. Sprinkle generously with additional Parmesan cheese. Cover with foil and bake for approximately 45 minutes, or until hot and bubbly. Remove from oven and let rest 15–20 minutes before cutting.

Serving suggestion: Serve with a tossed green salad with anchovy dressing (page 187).

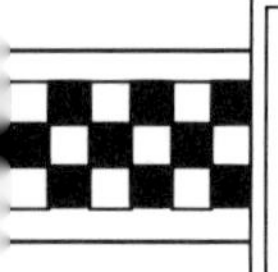

Pasta e Piselli (Pasta and Peas)

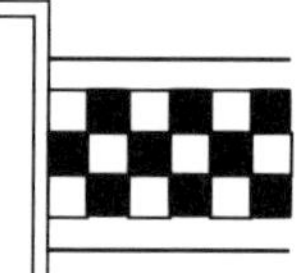

From Little Italy **Italian** ***Serves 4***

This pasta dish is enhanced with the flavor of prosciutto, a lightly cured Italian ham. If prosciutto is unavailable, a boiled or smoked ham can be used.

1 medium onion, minced
3 tablespoons olive oil
2 ounces prosciutto, diced
1 28-ounce can Italian plum tomatoes, drained and chopped
10-ounce package frozen peas or 1 cup fresh peas
1/4 cup chopped fresh parsley
Salt and freshly ground pepper to taste
1 pound penne (or your favorite shaped pasta)
1/2 cup freshly grated Parmesan

1. In a skillet, gently sauté onion in oil for 10 minutes. Add prosciutto and cook 2–3 minutes longer. Stir in tomatoes, fresh peas, parsley, salt and pepper and cook approximately 20 minutes, or until peas are tender. (If using frozen peas add at the last minute and cook 2–3 minutes.
2. Cook pasta until al dente. Drain. Place in a serving bowl, sprinkle with cheese and toss with the hot sauce.

Serving suggestion: Serve with a tossed salad and Italian bread (page 200).

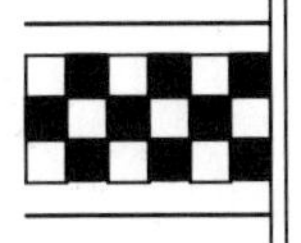

Pasta with Red Pepper Sauce

From Little Italy **Italian** ***Serves 4***

The combination of puréed peppers and onions creates the taste and texture of a tomato sauce. This is a delicious alternative to the more traditional pasta sauces.

1/4 cup olive oil
6 large red bell peppers, cored and thinly sliced
Salt and freshly ground pepper to taste
2 medium onions, sliced
1 cup chicken stock (preferably homemade, page 32)
1 pound pasta
Freshly grated Romano cheese to taste

1. In a skillet, heat oil over medium heat and sauté peppers. Add salt and pepper to taste. Reduce heat and cook peppers until softened, about 15–20 minutes. Add sliced onions and continue cooking until peppers and onions are thoroughly cooked and very soft.
2. Meanwhile cook pasta until al dente, drain and reserve.
3. Place pepper mixture in a food processor fitted with a steel blade and purée. Return pepper purée to skillet, add chicken stock and cook until heated through and slightly reduced. Adjust seasoning.
4. Place red pepper sauce over pasta, sprinkle with freshly grated cheese and serve at once.

Serving suggestions: Serve with a mixed green salad. If served as a side course, it is excellent as an accompaniment to grilled veal chops (page 67).

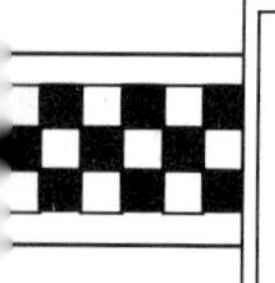

Shrimp with Linguine

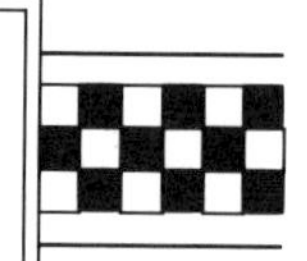

From Inner Harbor ***Serves 4***

This dish is best prepared with fresh herbs. If using dried, reduce the quantity by half.

3 tablespoons unsalted butter
3 scallions, chopped
1 garlic clove, minced
1 tablespoon chopped fresh basil
1 tablespoon chopped fresh thyme
1 tablespoon chopped fresh oregano
Salt and freshly ground pepper to taste
1/2 cup sliced mushrooms
1/2 pound small shrimp, peeled and deveined
1/2 cup clam juice or white wine
1 pound linguine

1. In a skillet, melt butter, add scallions, garlic and herbs and cook about 5–8 minutes. Add mushrooms and shrimp and sauté until shrimp are light pink in color. Pour in clam juice or wine and simmer another 2–3 minutes.

2. Meanwhile cook linguine until al dente. Drain. Place in a bowl and pour shrimp sauce over pasta. Toss thoroughly and serve.

Serving suggestion: Serve with a salad and Italian bread (page 200).

Variation: Serve with steamed clams and lobster meat. Sautéed scallops can be added to this pasta dish.

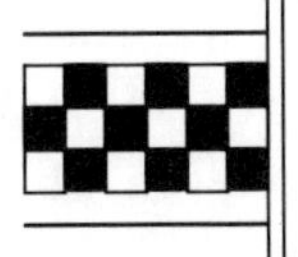

Basmati Rice

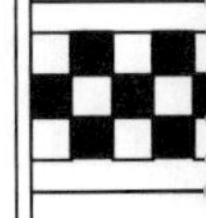

From Charles Center **Indian** ***Serves 4–6***

Basmati rice grows in the foothills of the Himalayas and is usually aged for a year before being sold. It is a long-grained rice and has a nutty aroma.

1 3/4 cups basmati rice
Pinch of salt
1 tablespoon unsalted butter
4 cups water

1. Rinse rice in strainer.
2. In a saucepan, combine rice, salt and butter. Add water, bring to a simmer, cover and cook over very low heat for 20 minutes, or until liquid has evaporated. Fluff rice with a fork, cover and simmer another 5–10 minutes, or until tender. Serve.

Serving suggestion: Serve with chicken tikka masala (page 76) and palak paneer (page 156).

Variation: To the simmering rice, add 1 or 2 whole cardamom pods and 1 whole cinnamon stick. Remove before serving.

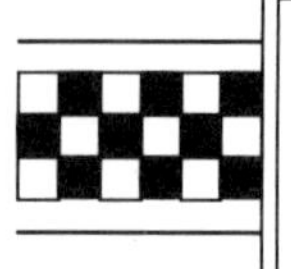

Rice Pilaf

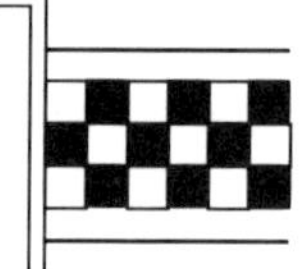

From Reservoir Hill **Middle Eastern** ***Serves 4***

The technique of coating rice with butter prevents it from sticking or clumping during cooking and results in a light, fluffy texture.

1 medium onion, minced
2–3 tablespoons unsalted butter
1 cup rice
2 1/2 cups chicken broth
Salt and pepper to taste

1. In a saucepan, sauté onion in melted butter until softened.
2. Add rice and toss in butter to coat.
3. Pour in chicken broth, bring to a boil, reduce heat and simmer uncovered for approximately 25 minutes, or until liquid is absorbed and rice is cooked. Remove from heat and let rice stand 3–4 minutes. Toss rice gently with a fork before serving.

Serving suggestions: Serve with veal with white wine sauce (page 65) or chicken with white wine, lemon and walnuts (page 71).

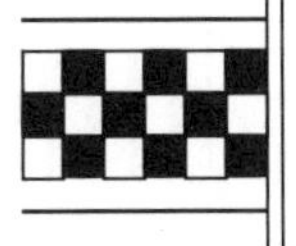

Spanish Rice

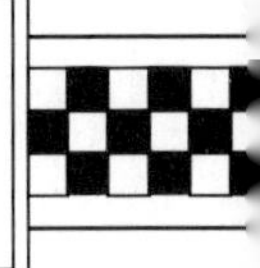

From Bolton **Spanish** ***Serves 6–8***

Saffron comes from the flower of a crocus; because of the small yield it is expensive. Saffron has a pungent bitter-honey taste and should be used in small amounts. It is best to steep saffron in hot water or stock. The strained liquid will be a light golden color with a delicate flavor of saffron, which is then used in many Mediterranean and Indian rice dishes.

2 teaspoons saffron
2 cups warm water
2 cups rice
1/4 cup olive oil
1/8 teaspoon chili powder
1 teaspoon garlic salt
1 cup Italian plum tomatoes, chopped, plus 1 cup juice from can

1. In a bowl, steep the saffron in 2 cups warm water.
2. In a skillet, add rice and oil and sauté gently 1 minute. Add chili powder and garlic salt. Pour in tomatoes and juice together with the saffron mixture and stir. Lower heat to simmer, cover and cook for approximately 35 minutes, or until rice is cooked and liquid has been absorbed.

Serving suggestions: Top with chorizo (page 102) or serve with veal in white wine sauce (page 65). Also excellent with meatloaf surprise (page 61).

Dressings and Sauces

Bolton Hill

Bolton Hill is believed to be where F. Scott Fitzgerald lived while finishing his novel *Tender Is the Night.* He was the great nephew of Francis Sott Key, who composed "The Star Spangled Banner" while looking toward the city's besieged Fort McHenry in 1814.

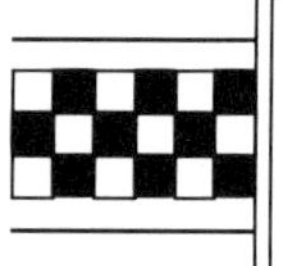

Cocktail Sauce

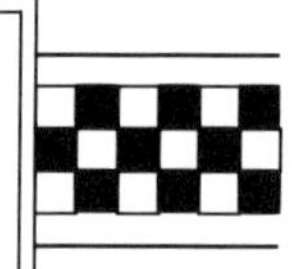

From Clifton Park ***Makes 1 cup***

A tasty sauce for your favorite shrimp or crab dishes.

1 cup tomato ketchup
1 tablespoon fresh horseradish sauce
1 teaspoon lemon juice
1/2 teaspoon Worcestershire sauce

1. In a bowl, whisk all ingredients together until well blended.
2. Chill before serving.

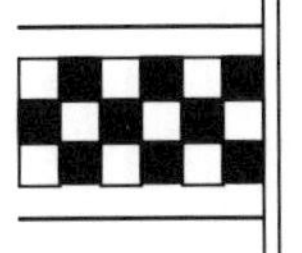

Horseradish Sauce

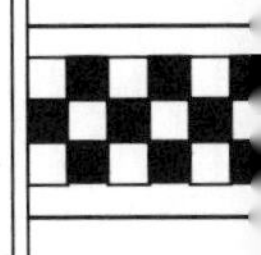

From Locust Point ***Makes 1 cup***

Fresh horseradish should be trimmed and scraped clean before grating.

1 cup sour cream
2 tablespoons fresh horseradish
1 tablespoon Dijon mustard
1 teaspoon Worcestershire sauce

1. In a bowl, mix all ingredients together. Whisk until smooth.
2. Chill for several hours before serving.

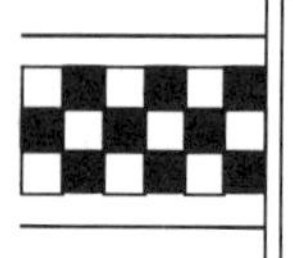

Anchovy Dressing

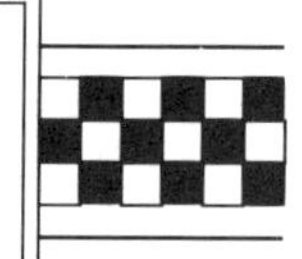

From Union Square **_Makes about 1/2 cup_**

Balsamic vinegar is made from the white Trebbiano grape of Italy. It is aged in wooden vats, which imparts a distinctive flavor. This is one of the few vinegars that can be used without oil for a dressing. It can also be sprinkled on strawberries and served for dessert.

2 tablespoons Balsamic vinegar
1/2 teaspoon anchovy paste
1/2 teaspoon Dijon mustard
1/3 cup olive oil

1. In a bowl, add Balsamic vinegar, anchovy paste and Dijon mustard.
2. Pour in olive oil in a slow, steady stream, whisking until smooth and creamy.

Tomato Vinaigrette

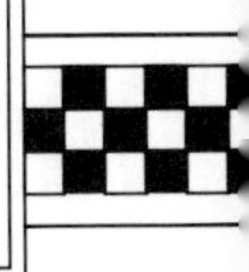

From Sowebo ***Makes about 1 cup***

Cumin (comino) is sold ground or as whole seeds. It is used extensively in Middle Eastern and Latin American dishes. Ground cumin adds a spicy but not a hot flavor to this vinaigrette.

2 ripe tomatoes, peeled and seeded
2 tablespoons red wine vinegar
1 garlic clove
1/8 teaspoon ground cumin
1/3 cup olive oil
Salt and freshly ground pepper to taste

1. In a food processor or blender, purée the tomatoes until smooth.
2. Add the vinegar, garlic and cumin and whiz. Gradually pour in olive oil and blend until smooth. Add salt and freshly ground pepper to taste.

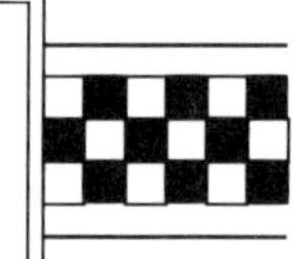

Tomato Sauce

From Bolton Hill ***Makes 5 cups***

Here is a wonderful way to use up the abundance of tomatoes during the summer. This recipe can be doubled and frozen to be used during the winter. Canned Italian plum tomatoes can be substituted for fresh if desired.

3 tablespoons olive oil
1 onion, finely chopped
1 carrot, finely chopped
1 celery stalk, finely chopped
4–5 pounds ripe tomatoes, peeled and crushed, or 1 28-ounce can Italian plum tomatoes, crushed
2 garlic cloves, minced
2 tablespoons finely chopped parsley
1 bay leaf
1 tablespoon oregano
Salt and pepper to taste

1. Heat oil in a large, non-metallic saucepan. Add the onion, carrot and celery and simmer until soft, stirring occasionally.
2. Add the tomatoes, garlic, parsley, bay leaf and oregano. Cover with lid slightly askew and simmer for about 1 hour, stirring occasionally. Remove bay leaf and add salt and pepper to taste.
3. For a smooth consistency, purée in a food processor or blender and sieve through a strainer or food mill.

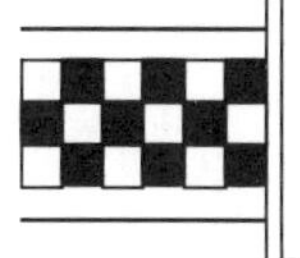

Tartar Sauce

From Sowebo ***Makes 1 cup***

Capers are grown in Mediterranean countries and are usually pickled in vinegar or dried and salted. They add a wonderful, piquant flavor to many sauces and are particularly good with seafood.

1 cup mayonnaise
2 teaspoons minced scallions
2 teaspoons capers plus 1 teaspoon juice from jar
1 teaspoon finely diced cornichons
1 tablespoon white wine vinegar
1 tablespoon minced parsley

1. In a bowl, combine all ingredients and mix until well blended.
2. Chill before serving.

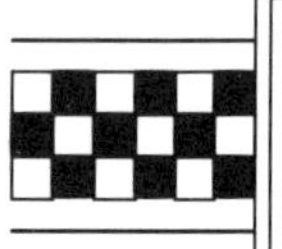

Cranberry Sauce

From Brooklyn ***Makes 3 cups***

Fresh cranberries are usually available from September until January. Cranberries freeze well, so you can always have an abundant supply ready in your freezer.

1 cup water
2 cups cranberries, coarsely chopped
1/2 cup sugar
1 orange, cut into pieces (do not remove skin)

1. Rinse cranberries thoroughly. In a saucepan, bring 1 cup of water to a boil, add cranberries and sugar and cook for about 10 minutes. Skim off any white froth that rises to the surface.
2. Add chopped orange pieces, stir to mix, pour into a serving dish and let cool. Sauce can be refrigerated for up to a week.

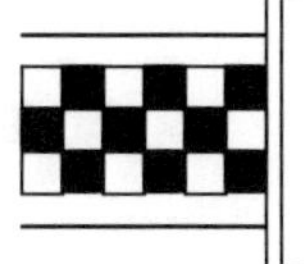

Chutney

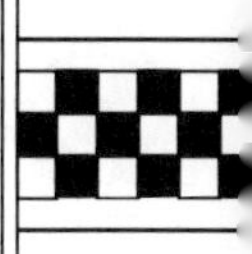

From Charles Center ***Makes 6–8 cups***

Chutney has a long shelf life. Kept in a cool, dark cupboard, it will mature with age. Malt vinegar has a pungent, mellow flavor that goes well with pickling. Its dark color gives this chutney its rich, dark, glossy look.

- 1 pound brown sugar
- 1 large onion, finely chopped
- 4 tart apples, peeled, cored and finely chopped
- 4 cups malt vinegar
- 1/3 cup chopped dates
- 1/3 cup chopped crystallized ginger
- 1/2 cup raisins
- 1/2 teaspoon cayenne pepper or paprika
- 1/4 teaspoon nutmeg
- 1/4 teaspoon dry mustard
- 1/2 teaspoon salt

1. In a large saucepan, add onions, apples and vinegar. Bring to a boil and simmer for 25 minutes.
2. Add remaining ingredients and cook slowly, stirring occasionally, until mixture is thick and syrupy, about 1–1 1/2 hours.
3. Pour into sterilized jars, cool, cover with top and store in a cool place—do not refrigerate. Let mature for at least 1 month before using.

Serving suggestions: Serve with curries, cold meats, add to mayonnaise or yogurt for a quick dip.

Parmesan Salad Dressing

From Roland Park ***Makes 1 quart***

The full recipe should be made for best results. This dressing is so delicious, you'll want to give some to a friend as a gift. Any leftover dressing should be refrigerated and used within a day or so.

- 2 3/4 cups olive oil
- 1/2 cup freshly squeezed lemon juice
- 1 cup freshly grated Parmesan cheese
- 2 tablespoons Worcestershire sauce
- 1 1/4 teaspoons cracked black pepper
- 2/3 teaspoon garlic salt
- 2 eggs, beaten

1. In a blender or food processor, combine all ingredients.

2. Whiz thoroughly until thick and smooth.

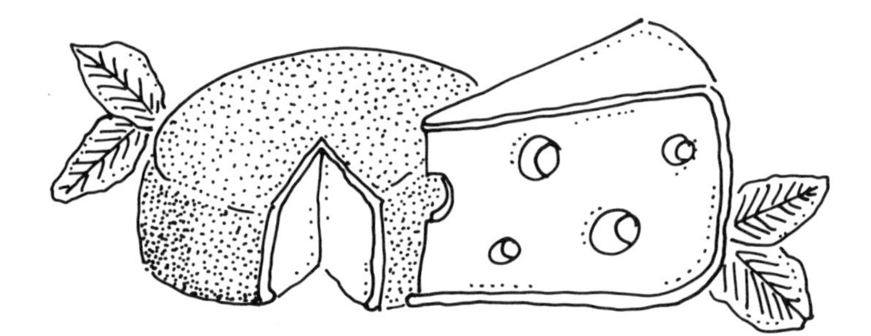

Breads, Pizza and Sandwiches

Otterbein

Otterbein is home to the Old Otterbein United Methodist Church. It is one of the city's oldest churches, built in 1785–86 by Jacob Small. Philip Wilhelm Otterbein served as pastor in this neighborhood from 1774 to 1813, and thus the church bears his name.

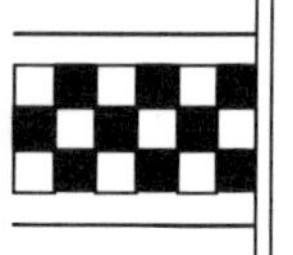

Zucchini Bread

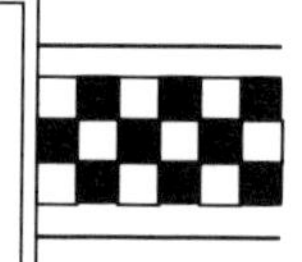

From Patterson Park ***Makes 1 loaf***

This is another good, moist and tasty version of zucchini bread. The orange zest adds a light citrus flavoring.

2 medium zucchini, washed, dried, ends trimmed and grated unpeeled (about 1 1/2 cups)
1 1/2 cups flour
1/4 teaspoon salt
1/2 teaspoon baking powder
1/4 pound (1 stick) unsalted butter
1 cup sugar
2 eggs
1 teaspoon vanilla
1 teaspoon orange zest
1/2 teaspoon cinnamon
1/2 cup raisins, plumped in 2 tablespoons boiling water
1/2 cup coarsely chopped walnuts

1. With paper towel pat grated zucchini gently to remove excess moisture.
2. In a bowl, combine flour, salt and baking powder. Reserve.
3. In another bowl, cream butter, add sugar and beat until fluffy. Add eggs, vanilla, orange zest and cinnamon. Stir in raisins along with liquid.
4. Mix dry ingredients into creamed butter mixture and gently stir in zucchini and walnuts.
5. Preheat oven to 350°.
6. Grease an 8 1/2×4 1/2×2 1/2-inch loaf pan. Fill loaf pan with batter and bake for about 1 hour. Cool in pan on a wire rack. Remove and cool completely on rack before serving.

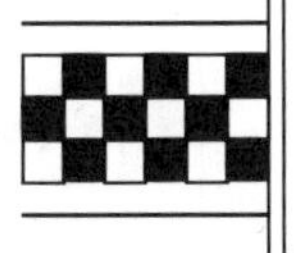

Sweet Potato Biscuits

From Upton ***Makes 10–12***

These biscuits are both light and delicious. The sweet potatoes give them a lovely yellow color and a slightly sweetish flavor. They freeze well and just need to be heated through before serving.

2 sweet potatoes, peeled, cubed and boiled
3/4 cup buttermilk
1 3/4 cups flour
1 tablespoon baking powder
Pinch of salt
1/4 cup vegetable shortening

1. Preheat oven to 400°.
2. Mash cooked potatoes until smooth.
3. In a small bowl, mix the mashed potatoes and milk together until fully blended.
4. In another bowl, add flour, baking powder and salt. Cut in the shortening until mixture resembles coarse meal. Gradually add in the potato mixture and stir until a soft dough is formed. The dough will be quite sticky.
5. Place dough on a floured work surface, sprinkle a little more flour on top of dough and gently pat out to about a 3/4-inch thickness. The dough is really too sticky to roll. Cut rounds about 2 inches in diameter. Arrange on an ungreased baking sheet and bake until lightly browned, about 30 minutes. Serve warm.

Serving suggestion: Serve with Maryland fried chicken (page 75) or pork chop casserole (page 92).

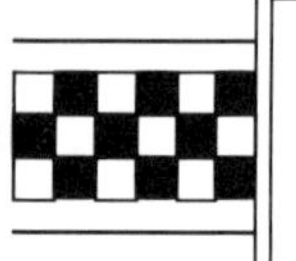

Oatcakes

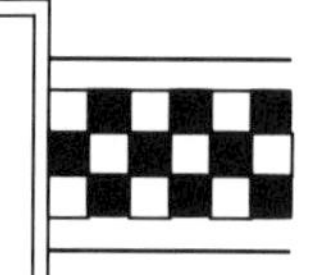

From Locust Point **Irish** ***Makes 2 6-inch cakes***

These traditional oatcakes are easy to make and are usually served warm with butter and jam for high tea or as a savory biscuit with cheese.

2 cups rolled oats
1/4 cup flour
1/2 teaspoon baking powder
1/4 teaspoon salt
4 tablespoons margarine, melted
1/2 cup hot water
Oat bran

1. Preheat oven to 350°.
2. In a blender or food processor, coarsely grind 1 cup of the rolled oats.
3. In a bowl, combine ground oats, remaining cup of oats, flour, baking powder and salt. Mix in margarine and toss with a fork. Pour hot water over mixture and stir until it forms a dough. Divide dough in half.
4. Sprinkle a work surface with oat bran and roll out 1 portion of dough into a circle about 6 inches in diameter. Place on an ungreased baking sheet. Repeat with remaining dough.
5. Bake for approximately 10–15 minutes. Turn oven off, leave door open and allow cakes to sit in oven for about 4–5 minutes to firm and crisp. Remove from oven, cut into wedges, cool completely and store in an air-tight container.

Serving suggestion: Serve with cheeses such as Cheddar, Stilton or your favorite aged or soft cheese.

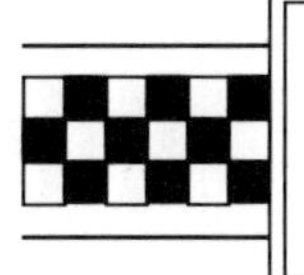

Italian Bread

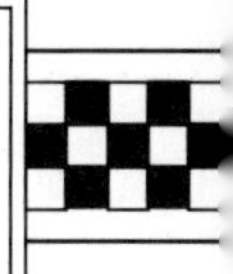

From Little Italy ***Makes 1 large or 2 small loaves***

This recipe makes a crispy, crusty loaf of bread which also freezes well.

1 1/2 packets active yeast
2 1/2 cups warm water
2 1/2 pounds flour
8–9 cups flour
1 1/2 teaspoons salt
1/4 cup vegetable oil

1. Proof yeast in 1/2 cup warm water until foamy, about 5 minutes.
2. Mix flour and salt together and place on a work surface. Make a well, add the yeast mixture and with hands draw a little flour into the mixture. Gradually pour remaining water into the well, slowly incorporating as much of the remaining flour as needed to form a dough.
3. Oil hands and knead dough about 10 minutes, or until smooth and elastic. Place in a greased bowl and cover with a damp towel. Let rise in a warm place about 2 hours, or until double.
4. Punch dough down and shape into freeform loaves. Place on a greased jellyroll pan and let rise 1 hour.
5. Preheat oven to 375°.
6. Bake for 1 hour. To test for doneness, the bread should sound hollow when tapped.

Serving suggestions: Serve with clam chowder (page 31) or marinated broiled scallops (page 127).

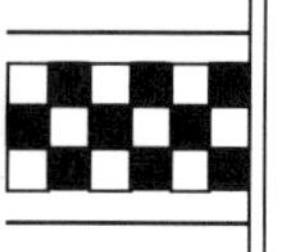

Cornbread

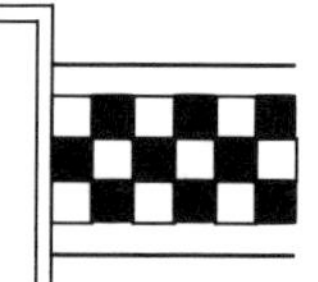

From Upton **African American** ***Makes 6 wedges***

For a moist center and crispy crust, place a pan of water on bottom of oven while baking cornbread. This will add a little steam to the oven and will give the crust a crisp finish.

1 cup yellow cornmeal
1 cup flour
Pinch of sugar
4 teaspoons baking powder
1 teaspoon salt
2 eggs
1 cup milk
1/4 cup vegetable oil

1. Preheat oven to 425°.
2. Sift dry ingredients into a mixing bowl. Add egg, milk and oil and beat until smooth.
3. Grease an 8- or 9-inch skillet or square baking pan, pour in batter and bake for 25–30 minutes until golden brown. Cut into wedges and serve.

Serving suggestions: Serve with any thick soup or with Maryland kidney stew (page 99).

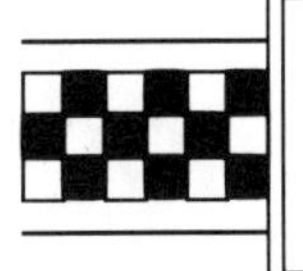

Beaten Biscuits

From Lexington Market **Makes 6–8**

Beaten biscuits are a Southern specialty, and traditionally the dough was repeatedly pounded with a hammer or mallet before being baked. Today the food processor can perform this job quite successfully. The biscuits can be frozen, but be sure to warm them before serving.

1 cup flour
1/4 cup vegetable shortening
1/4 teaspoon salt
1/4 teaspoon baking soda
1/4 teaspoon sugar
1/2–3/4 cup water

1. Preheat oven to 400°.
2. In a food processor or mixer, add all ingredients except water and whiz to blend.
3. Slowly add just enough water to form a soft dough. Remove dough and divide into 6 parts. Place each piece of dough one at a time in a processor or mixer and beat for about 1 minute. (The dough will first separate, but will reform into a ball again after a few seconds of beating.)
4. On a floured surface, knead together all the beaten dough balls until smooth. Break off pieces of dough and with lightly floured hands, form into 1-inch balls. Place on a lightly buttered baking dish and flatten slightly with fork, pricking the top 2–3 times. Bake 20 minutes, or until lightly golden in color. Serve warm or reheat before serving.

Serving suggestions: Serve with clam chowder (page 31).

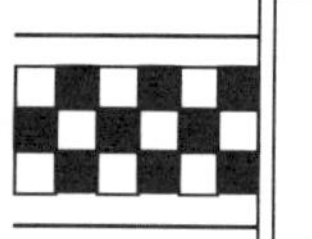

Baltimore Cheese Bread

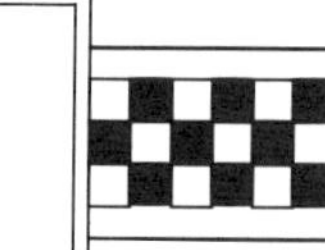

From Inner Harbor ***Makes 1 loaf, 12 servings***

This bread was created by the original owner of "Ms. Desserts." It can be frozen and is best when reheated and served warm.

1/4 cup plus 1 teaspoon sugar
3 tablespoons water, warmed
1 package (1/4 ounce) active dry yeast
2 eggs
1 cup milk
1/2 cup (1 stick) unsalted butter, melted and cooled to room temperature
1 teaspoon salt
About 5 cups flour
1 pound (4 cups) Jarlsberg, Svenbo or Swiss cheese, grated
1 egg lightly beaten for glaze

---

1. In a small bowl, stir 1 teaspoon of sugar into 3 tablespoons of warm water. Stir in yeast and set aside until proofed, about 10 minutes.

2. In a large bowl, lightly beat eggs and mix in the remaining sugar, milk, butter and salt. Blend in yeast mixture and then stir in 2 cups of the flour to make a dough. Add in another 1 1/2 cups flour, turn the dough onto a work surface and knead in enough of the remaining flour to make a soft, smooth dough. Knead about 15 minutes more, or until it is smooth and satiny.

3. Place dough in a lightly oiled bowl, turning it lightly to grease the surface. Cover with a towel and allow to rise in a warm place about 1 1/2 hours, or until double in bulk.

4. Thoroughly grease a 9-inch pie plate. Punch down the dough and roll it into a 16-inch round. Center the dough in the pie plate, pressing it snugly against the edges of the plate and allowing the excess dough to hang over. Mound the cheese in the center and fold and pleat the dough into a turban shape by gathering it into 6 or 7 equally spaced folds, stretching the dough slightly as you draw each pleat over the filling. Holding the ends of the dough in your hand, twist them together tightly on top to form a little topknot. Glaze the surface by brushing it with the lightly beaten egg, set it aside in a warm place and let rise about 45 minutes, or until double in bulk.

5. Preheat oven to 325°.

6. Bake the bread in the center of the oven for about 50 minutes, or until the top is golden brown and the bread sounds hollow when lightly tapped on the side. Cool for 15 minutes, remove from pan and let rest another 30 minutes before slicing into wedges and serving.

Serving suggestions: Serve with soup, stew or salad.

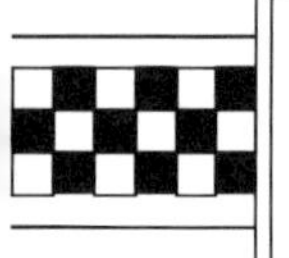

Lahmajoon (Armenian Pizza)

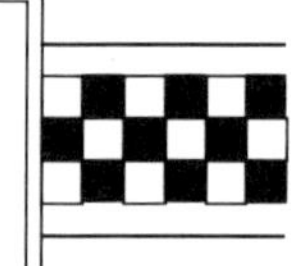

From Roland Park ***Makes about 2 1/2 dozen 6-inch pizzas***

For this recipe, it is not necessary to proof the yeast. Simply combine the yeast mixture into the flour immediately and proceed. The very tasty topping and the light-textured dough create an exceptional and unusual pizza.

DOUGH
1 cup lukewarm water
2 packages yeast
1/2 cup vegetable shortening, melted
4 1/2 cups all-purpose flour
1 teaspoon salt
1 teaspoon sugar

TOPPING
1 pound ground lamb
1 pound ground beef
2 garlic cloves, crushed
2 cups chopped parsley
2 cups chopped onions
1 cup chopped red peppers
1 cup chopped green peppers
1 6-ounce can tomato paste
2 16-ounce cans peeled tomatoes, drained and chopped
Salt, pepper and paprika to taste

1. To make dough, stir together water, yeast and shortening in a large bowl. Add flour, sugar and salt and with your hands, work the ingredients together until a soft dough forms. Turn onto a floured surface and knead until it is no longer sticky, about 10 minutes. (Hands should be lightly oiled before kneading dough. Dough should be smooth and elastic in texture after kneading.) Place dough in bowl, cover with a damp cloth and allow to rise for 2–3 hours in a warm place. After dough has risen, divide into 28 balls and roll each piece into a 6-inch circle.

2. While dough is rising, prepare topping. In a large bowl, combine all ingredients and mix thoroughly.

3. Preheat oven to 450°.

4. Spread a thin layer of mixture over the entire surface of each pizza. Place on a greased cookie sheet and bake 15 minutes, or until meat is cooked through. Serve warm.

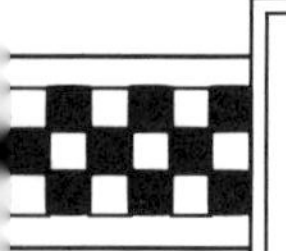

Courtyard Health Sandwich

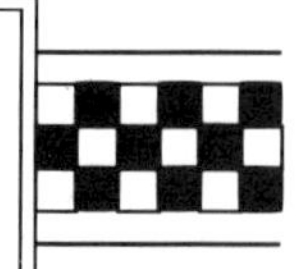

From Charles Center **Makes 4 sandwiches**

An interesting combination of textures and flavors makes this sandwich special and one you will want to enjoy time and time again. If bean sprouts seem gritty, rinse and make sure to pat them dry thoroughly before using.

1 recipe hommus (page 14)
8 slices whole wheat bread or
  4 whole pita
1 cup grated carrots
3 tomatoes, thinly sliced
1 cup bean sprouts
1 cup grated Gruyere cheese

1. Spread hommus generously on one slice of bread or spoon into pita. Layer with remaining ingredients and top with second slice of bread.
2. Repeat for remaining sandwiches.

Boursin Chicken Sandwich

From Inner Harbor ***Makes 4 sandwiches***

This sandwich can be prepared with your favorite herb-flavored soft cheese. Chicken should be sautéed gently and not overcooked for it to be tender, juicy and succulent.

- 2 whole chicken breasts, split, boned, skinned and flattened
- 4 tablespoons unsalted butter
- 1/2 cup garlic-flavored soft cheese (Boursin, Alouette, Rondelé, etc.)
- 4 egg rolls, warmed and split (Kaiser rolls, pita bread or French bread may be used.)

1. In a skillet, heat butter. Add chicken breasts and sauté until just cooked, about 5 minutes on each side.
2. Spread about 2 tablespoons of cheese over each chicken piece, cover skillet and cook 1 minute, or until cheese has melted slightly.
3. Place chicken in rolls and serve.

Desserts

Old Town

Old Town is the home of the world-famous John Hopkins Hospital, named after one of the city's great magnates. A stone's throw away is Belair, another of Baltimore's excellent food markets.

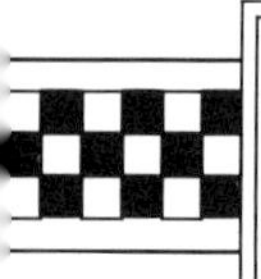

Karidopita (Walnut Wine Cake)

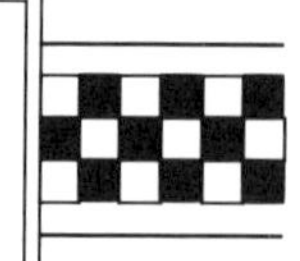

From Fells Point **Greek** ***Makes 22 pieces***

To cut this cake into diamond shapes, slice lengthwise evenly 3 times. Then cut widthwise on the diagonal at about 3-inch intervals.

6 eggs, separated
1 cup granulated sugar
1/4 teaspoon ground cinnamon
1 teaspoon grated orange peel
1/8 teaspoon cream of tartar
1 cup ground zwieback (approximately 12 zwieback) or cake flour
2 teaspoons baking powder
1/8 teaspoon salt
1 cup ground walnuts

HONEY WINE SYRUP
1 cup honey
1/2 cup water
1 teaspoon orange juice
1/2 cup port wine

1. Preheat oven to 350°.
2. In a bowl, beat egg yolks until thick and lemon-colored. Add sugar and continue beating. Beat in cinnamon and orange peel.
3. In a large bowl, beat egg whites with cream of tartar until stiff. Fold yolk mixture gently into egg whites.
4. Combine ground zwieback or cake flour, baking powder and salt. Fold into egg white mixture. Mix in walnuts gently.
5. Pour batter into a buttered 9×13×2-inch pan and bake for approximately 35–40 minutes.

6. Just before removing cake from oven, prepare honey wine syrup. In a medium saucepan, bring honey, water, orange juice and wine to a boil. Remove cake from oven and very slowly pour hot syrup evenly over hot cake. Allow cake to absorb syrup for several hours.
7. With a sharp knife, cut cake into diamond-shaped pieces before serving.

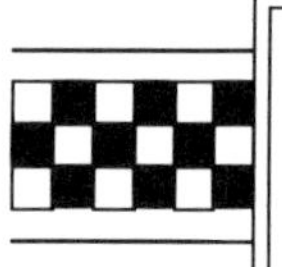

Strawberry Shortcake

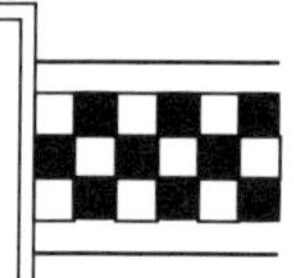

From Southeast Baltimore ***Serves 6–8***

Some strawberry shortcakes are made with a biscuit dough, but this particular version is made with a yellow cake, generously filled and topped with whipped cream and strawberries.

Butter for greasing
Flour for dusting

CAKE

1 cup plus 2 tablespoons all-purpose flour
1 1/4 teaspoons baking powder
1/4 teaspoon salt
4 tablespoons (1/2 stick) unsalted butter
3/4 cup granulated sugar
1/2 teaspoon vanilla
1/4 teaspoon Amaretto liqueur or almond extract
1 egg
1/2 cup milk

2 pints strawberries, cleaned and hulled
1/4 cup plus 2 tablespoons granulated sugar
1 cup heavy whipping cream

1. Grease and flour an 8-inch cake pan.
2. Preheat oven to 375°.
3. In a bowl, combine flour, baking powder and salt.
4. In another bowl, beat butter, add sugar, vanilla and Amaretto and continue beating until well mixed. Add egg and beat 1 minute.
5. To the butter mixture, stir in the dry ingredients, alternating with milk until blended. Pour into prepared pan and bake for 30–35 minutes. Cool 10 minutes in pan on wire rack, remove from pan and cool completely. With a serrated knife, slice cake in half horizontally.

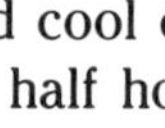

6. Place strawberries in a bowl and toss with 1/4 cup of the sugar. Set aside for about 20 minutes.
7. Whip heavy cream with the remaining 2 tablespoons of sugar until stiff.
8. To assemble, spoon half the strawberry mixture with accumulated juice evenly on bottom half of cake and top with half the whipped cream. Top with remaining cake and spoon remaining whipped cream evenly over cake. Place remaining strawberries into whipped cream topping. Chill slightly before serving.

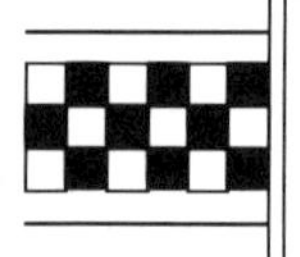

Apple Cake

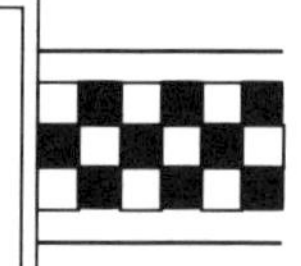

From South Baltimore **Jewish** ***Serves 8–10***

A delicious yet easy recipe for a traditional favorite. Apple cake can also be made by mixing the apples carefully into the batter before cooking.

4–5 tart apples, peeled and thinly sliced
2 teaspoons ground cinnamon
2 1/2 cups granulated sugar
4 eggs
1/2 cup orange juice
1 cup vegetable oil
3 cups all-purpose flour
1/2 teaspoon salt
1 tablespoon baking powder
2 1/2 teaspoons vanilla
Butter

1. In a bowl, combine apples with cinnamon and 1/4 cup of the sugar. Reserve.
2. Preheat oven to 350°.
3. In a large bowl, mix together eggs, remaining 2 1/4 cups sugar, orange juice, oil, flour, salt and baking powder. Add vanilla and stir to combine.
4. Butter a 10-inch bundt or tube pan. Pour half of the batter into the pan, then add half of the apple mixture. Pour remaining batter over apples and top with remaining apple mixture.
5. Bake for approximately 1 3/4 hours. Cool before serving.

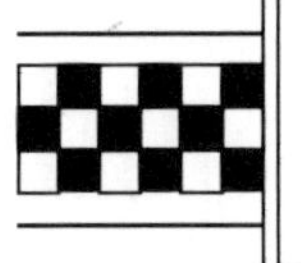

Piernik Wyborny (Fruit Cake)

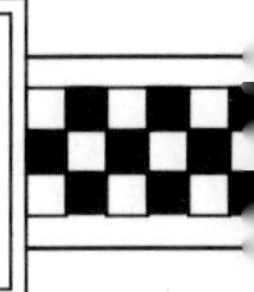

From Howard Park **Polish** ***Serves 8***

This is a very dense and rich traditional Polish Christmas cake.

1 1/2 cups honey
1 cup granulated sugar
1 package yeast
1/2 cup beer, room temperature
1 tablespoon butter, softened
4 eggs, beaten
4 cups flour
Pinch of black pepper
1/2 teaspoon ground cloves
1/2 teaspoon ground cinnamon
1/2 cup dried figs, chopped
1/2 cup walnuts, chopped
1/2 cup dates, chopped
2 tablespoons orange peel

1. In a large saucepan, bring honey to the boiling point. Add sugar and return to a boil. Remove from heat and cool slightly for 10 minutes.
2. Preheat oven to 350°.
3. In a small bowl, add the yeast and pour in beer. Allow to sit a few minutes until yeast has dissolved and is bubbly.
4. Add the yeast mixture to the honey and stir. Add butter and eggs and mix in the flour one cup at a time. The mixture will be fairly thick at this point.
5. Stir in remaining ingredients thoroughly.
6. Butter an 8×8-inch baking pan. Spread batter evenly in pan and bake for 40 minutes. Remove from oven, cool slightly and cut into desired pieces.

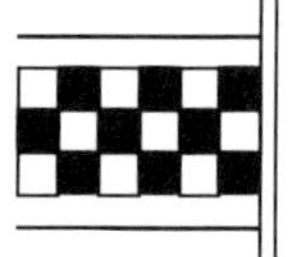

Baltimore Cheesecake

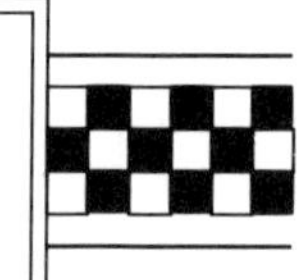

From Hollins Market, Sowebo ***Serves 8–10***

This cheesecake may also be made using the lighter Neufchatel cream cheese. For a special treat, top with your favorite fruit or chocolate curls.

GRAHAM CRACKER CRUST

1 3/4 cups graham cracker crumbs
6 tablespoons butter or margarine, melted
1/4 cup granulated sugar

FILLING

1 pound cream cheese
1 pint sour cream
1 cup granulated sugar
2 teaspoons cornstarch
2 teaspoons lemon juice
1 teaspoon vanilla
Pinch of salt
4 eggs, beaten until fluffy

1. To make crust, combine graham cracker crumbs with butter and sugar and press into the bottom and half-way up the sides of an 8-inch springform pan. Set aside.
2. Preheat oven to 350°.
3. To make filling, beat cream cheese until soft, add sour cream and beat until smooth. Add sugar and continue beating until sugar has dissolved. Mix in remaining ingredients until thoroughly blended. Pour into prepared crust.
4. Bake 50–60 minutes. Cake center will be underdone and will jiggle slightly. Turn off oven and allow cake to sit in oven 60 minutes with oven door slightly ajar. Cake will continue cooking and will set at this point. Cool completely and refrigerate overnight.
5. To serve, remove sides of springform and place on serving platter.

Cranapple Compote

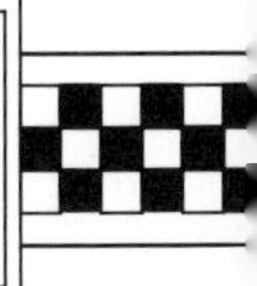

From Walbrook **Serves 6–8**

This makes an excellent hostess gift when poured into attractive Mason jars.

1 1/2 cups plus 2 tablespoons water
3/4 cup frozen apple juice concentrate
1 teaspoon vanilla
1 teaspoon lemon juice
1 12-ounce bag cranberries
4 Granny Smith apples, peeled, cored and sliced
2 tablespoons cornstarch

1. In a saucepan, bring 1 1/2 cups water, apple juice, vanilla and lemon juice to a boil. Add the cranberries and apples, bring back to a boil, reduce heat and simmer uncovered for 10–15 minutes.
2. In a small bowl, add the remaining 2 tablespoons of water plus cornstarch and stir until mixed.
3. When cranberries and apples are cooked, stir in the cornstarch mixture and cook until thickened. Remove from heat, cool and chill in refrigerator before serving.

Serving suggestions: Serve with vanilla ice cream or plain yogurt. Also excellent as an accompaniment to turkey or stuffed quail (page 94).

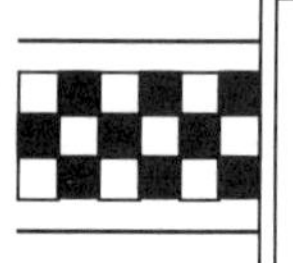

Blueberry Coffee Cake

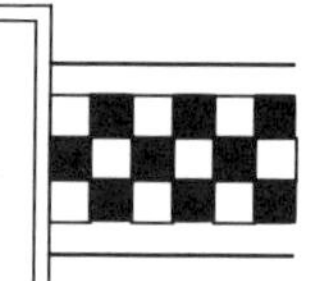

From Windsor Hills

As blueberries freeze well, purchase them when they are abundant for future use.

Butter
Flour for dusting pan
3/4 cup granulated sugar
1/4 cup vegetable shortening
1 egg
1/2 cup milk
2 cups all-purpose flour
1/2 teaspoon salt
2 teaspoons baking powder
2 cups blueberries

CRUMB TOPPING
1/2 cup granulated sugar
1/3 cup all-purpose flour
1/2 teaspoon ground cinnamon
1/4 cup (4 tablespoons) margarine, room temperature

1. Heat oven to 375°.
2. Butter and flour a 9-inch square baking dish.
3. In a bowl, mix together sugar, shortening and egg. Stir in milk. Add flour, salt and baking powder and mix to combine. Carefully fold in blueberries. Spread mixture in baking dish.
4. Prepare crumb topping. In a bowl, mix sugar, flour and cinnamon. Cut in margarine until mixture resembles coarse crumbs.
5. Sprinkle crumb topping over blueberry mixture and bake 45–50 minutes, or until a toothpick inserted in center comes out clean.
6. Cool completely, cut into squares and serve.

Baltimore Butter Cake

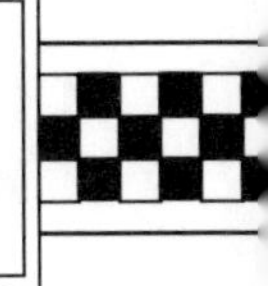

From Arlington ***Serves 10–12***

A nice addition to the butter sauce is a sprinkling of Amaretto or rum before pouring over cake.

Vegetable shortening to grease pan
Flour for dusting pan

CAKE
3 cups all-purpose flour
2 cups granulated sugar
1 teaspoon salt
1 teaspoon baking powder
1/2 teaspoon baking soda
1 cup (2 sticks) butter, room temperature
2 teaspoons vanilla
4 eggs

BUTTER SAUCE
6 tablespoons butter
3/4 cup granulated sugar
3 tablespoons water
2 teaspoons vanilla

1. Preheat oven to 325°.
2. Generously grease a 10-inch tube pan and dust lightly with flour.
3. In a food processor or mixer, blend cake ingredients together until moistened and beat an additional 2–3 minutes. Pour batter into prepared pan and bake for 60–70 minutes, or until a toothpick inserted in center comes out clean.
4. Meanwhile prepare sauce. In a small saucepan, combine ingredients and heat until butter melts. Do not bring mixture to a boil.
5. When cake is cooked, remove from oven and with a long-tined fork, pierce hot cake 10–12 times. Slowly pour hot butter sauce over cake. Cool in pan 30–40 minutes. Remove from pan and serve.

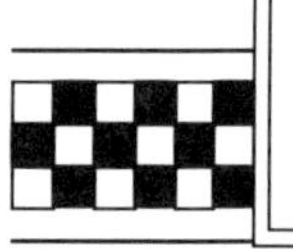

Pastiera di Granno (Easter Wheat Pie)

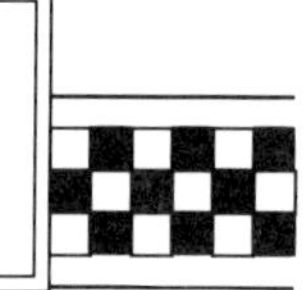

From Little Italy **Italian** ***Serves 8***

This is a traditional Neapolitan pastry served at Easter which is time-consuming to make, but worth the effort. Wheat grain has a nutty flavor and gives a wonderful taste and texture to this pie.

3/4 cup whole grain wheat, soaked in water for 2–3 days
1 1/2 cups milk

PASTRY
2 cups all-purpose flour
1/3 cup granulated sugar
4 tablespoons (1/2 stick) unsalted butter
4 eggs
1/4 cup milk

FILLING
2 cups ricotta
3 eggs, separated
1/3 cup granulated sugar
1 teaspoon orange flower water
1/2 orange, unpeeled and finely chopped
1/2 lemon, unpeeled and finely chopped
1/2 teaspoon vanilla

1. Drain the soaked wheat. In a saucepan, combine wheat and milk and simmer gently for about 1–1 1/2 hours until wheat is soft and has absorbed the milk. (Mixture should be stirred occasionally to prevent sticking.) Reserve.
2. To make pastry, combine flour and sugar in a bowl. Cut in butter until mixture resembles coarse crumbs. Add eggs, one at a time, blending well. Add just enough milk until dough forms into a ball. Knead until smooth, wrap in plastic wrap and let rest for 10–15 minutes before rolling. Cut 1/4 of the pastry dough and set aside. On a floured surface, roll out remaining dough to fit a 9-inch pie pan. Set aside.

3. To make filling, in a bowl, combine ricotta, egg yolks, sugar, orange flower water, orange, lemon, vanilla and reserved wheat. With a fork, mix ingredients well.
4. Beat egg whites until stiff and gently fold into ricotta mixture. Pour mixture into prepared crust.
5. Preheat oven to 350°.
6. On a floured surface, roll out remaining pastry dough into a long, rectangular shape and with a fluted pastry wheel or knife, cut strips about 3/4-inch wide. Place strips lattice-style over filling and bake 1 hour, or until pastry is golden brown. Cool slightly and serve.

No-Crust Coconut Pie

From Mt. Washington/Cheswold ***Serves 6***

This pie is light and easy to make. Be sure to use unsweetened coconut for this dessert.

Butter for greasing
Flour for dusting
1/2 cup granulated sugar
2 eggs
1 cup milk
1/4 cup self-rising flour
3 ounces unsweetened coconut
1 teaspoon vanilla

1. Preheat oven to 325°.
2. Butter an 8-inch pie plate and dust with flour.
3. In a food processor or large bowl, whisk together remaining ingredients until smooth. Pour into prepared pie plate and bake for 30 minutes, or until firm and golden in color. Serve warm or cold.

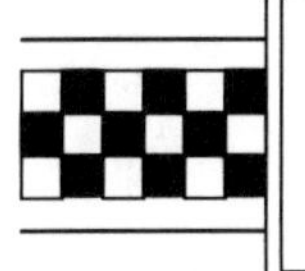

Linzer Torte

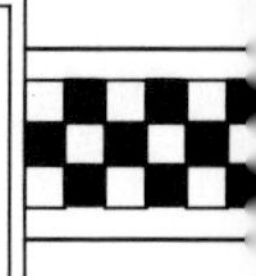

From Canton **German** ***Serves 6–8***

Allspice is ground from the dried berries of a tropical evergreen tree. It can be used with meats, sauces and sweet potatoes but more traditionally in desserts like spice cake and cookies. It has a subtle flavor suggestive of nutmeg, cloves and cinnamon. If desired this torte can be made with ground walnuts instead of almonds.

1 1/2 cups all-purpose flour
3/4 cup granulated sugar
1 teaspoon ground cinnamon
1 teaspoon allspice
8 tablespoons unsalted butter, softened
3/4 cup ground almonds
2 egg yolks
1/2 cup raspberry preserves

1. Preheat oven to 350°.
2. In a bowl, add 1 1/3 cups of the flour along with the sugar, cinnamon and allspice. Blend in butter and with a fork, mix thoroughly. Dough will be fairly soft. Stir in almonds and fold in egg yolks, one at a time. (The dough is still quite sticky at this point.)
3. In a 10-inch tart pan, spread 3/4 of the dough and with your fingers, press the dough evenly into the pan. Spread raspberry preserve evenly over crust.
4. Place remaining dough on a floured surface and knead in remaining flour so dough is no longer sticky and can be rolled out easily. (Dough is still quite fragile.) Roll dough into a rectangular shape and with a fluted pastry wheel or knife, cut into approximately 3/8-inch-wide strips. Place strips lattice-style over preserves.

Bake for 20–25 minutes, or until top pastry is lightly browned. Remove from oven and cool.

Serving suggestions: Serve with vanilla ice cream or unsweetened whipped cream.

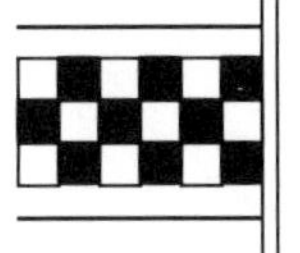

Fresh Fruit Tart

From Mt. Vernon ***Serves 6–8***

This tart is pretty as a picture and tastes spectacular. A kiwi and strawberry fruit topping is an especially good combination.

PASTRY SHELL

1 3/4 cups all-purpose flour
2 tablespoons granulated sugar
1/2 teaspoon salt
1 1/2 sticks unsalted butter, cut into pieces
1 egg yolk
3 tablespoons cold water

FILLING

1 cup plus 2 tablespoons heavy whipped cream
8 ounces cream cheese, room temperature
1/3 cup confectioner's sugar
1 teaspoon vanilla extract
3 tablespoons orange liqueur (optional)
6 ounces semi-sweet chocolate
Fresh fruit for topping: kiwi, strawberries, blueberries, etc.
1/2 cup apricot or peach jam, melted for glaze

1. Preheat oven to 375°.
2. Prepare pastry. In the bowl of a food processor or in a mixing bowl, combine flour, sugar and salt. Cut in butter until mixture resembles coarse crumbs. In another bowl, mix together egg yolk and cold water. Pour a little at a time into flour mixture until dough forms into a ball. If making by hand, use a fork to incorporate egg/water mixture into the flour. Remove and roll out dough on a lightly floured surface. Line a 10-inch tart pan with dough and place in freezer for 10 minutes. Bake approximately 25 minutes, or until lightly golden. Cool and set aside
3. In a bowl, whip 1 cup heavy cream until stiff. Reserve.

4. Beat cream cheese until soft and add sugar, vanilla and liqueur, if desired. Fold in whipped cream. Chill until ready to assemble.
5. Meanwhile melt chocolate in a heavy saucepan with the remaining 2 tablespoons heavy cream. Spread a thin layer over cooked tart shell. (Tart shell should not be hot from the oven, but cooled slightly before spreading chocolate layer.)
6. When chocolate layer has cooled, fill with cream cheese mixture.
7. Top decoratively with fresh fruit. Brush melted jam over fruit for glaze. Refrigerate tart several hours. Remove from refrigerator about 20 minutes before serving.

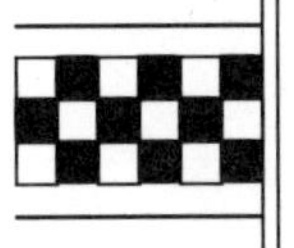

Southern Strawberry Tart

From Inner Harbor ***Serves 6–8***

For this spectacular tart, be sure to use large strawberries that are fairly uniform in size to make an eye-catching presentation.

1 9-inch tart shell, pre-baked (page 226)
1/3 cup granulated sugar
1 tablespoon cornstarch
1 tablespoon dark corn syrup
1/2 cup water
1 1/2 tablespoons strawberry flavored gelatin
2 pints strawberries, cleaned and stem ends cut off

1. In a saucepan, combine sugar, cornstarch, corn syrup and water. Bring to a boil, reduce heat and cook, stirring constantly, about 3 minutes, or until clear and slightly thickened. Remove from heat, add gelatin and stir until dissolved. Cool.
2. Place strawberries, cut side down, decoratively in prebaked tart shell. Spoon gelatin mixture evenly over strawberries. Place tart in refrigerator and chill several hours or overnight until firm.

Serving suggestions: Serve with unsweetened whipped cream or vanilla ice cream.

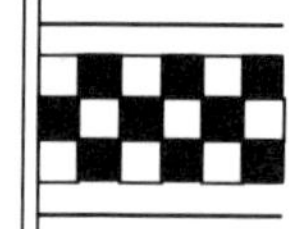

Oatmeal Chocolate Chunk Cookies

From Patterson Park ***Makes 2 dozen***

These cookies are exceptionally delicious. They may also be made with chocolate chips and with your favorite chocolate bar.

1/2 cup (1 stick) unsalted butter, room temperature
1/2 cup granulated sugar
1/2 cup brown sugar
1 egg
1/2 teaspoon vanilla
1 cup all-purpose flour
1 1/4 cups oatmeal, ground to powder
1/4 teaspoon salt
1/2 teaspoon baking powder
1/2 teaspoon baking soda
6 ounces semi-sweet baking chocolate, broken into 1/2-inch chunks
1 1/2-ounce milk chocolate bar with almonds, broken into 1/2-inch chunks

1. Preheat oven to 375°.
2. In a bowl, cream butter. Add granulated and brown sugar, beat until well incorporated. Add egg and vanilla, continue beating until smooth.
3. In another bowl, combine flour, oatmeal, salt, baking powder and baking soda.
4. Add dry ingredients to the butter mixture and mix thoroughly.
5. Stir in chocolate chunks.
6. Scoop cookie dough (about golf ball size) and place on an ungreased cookie sheet, about 2 inches apart. Bake 10–15 minutes.

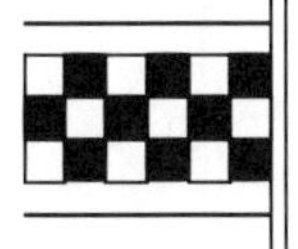

Layered Chocolate Brownies

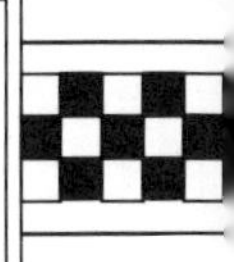

From Roland Park ***Makes 2–3 dozen bars***

A delicious, unusual and rich chocolate brownie with three layers. Care should be taken when spreading buttercream and chocolate glaze on brownies. The cake should be completely cool before spreading the buttercream layer.

CAKE

1/2 cup (1 stick) unsalted butter
1 cup granulated sugar
4 eggs, beaten
1 teaspoon vanilla
1 16-ounce can chocolate syrup
1 cup flour
1/2 teaspoon salt

BUTTERCREAM LAYER

1/2 cup butter
2 cups confectioner's sugar
2 tablespoons crème de menthe, crème de cacao or Kahlua

GLAZE

6 ounces semi-sweet chocolate chips
6 tablespoons butter

---

1. Preheat oven to 350°.
2. To make the cake, mix butter with sugar and add eggs, vanilla and chocolate syrup. Stir in flour and salt to combine. Pour into a greased 9×12-inch pan and bake for 25–30 minutes. Cool in pan.
3. To make buttercream layer, mix all ingredients thoroughly.
4. Spread buttercream mixture on cooled cake and refrigerate about 40 minutes.
5. Meanwhile prepare glaze. Melt chocolate and butter in a small saucepan on top of stove. Refrigerate 20 minutes until cool but spreadable.

6. Remove cake from refrigerator and carefully spread chocolate glaze over buttercream layer. Refrigerate again before cutting into bars.
7. Serve at room temperature.

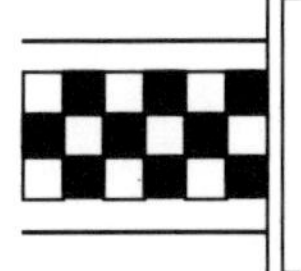

Piernik Gwaltu! Goscie Jada (Honey Cookies)

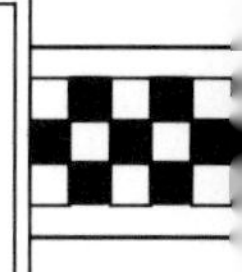

From Howard Park **Polish** ***Makes 2 1/2–3 dozen***

These cookies can be used for Christmas tree decorations by sprinkling them with different colored sugars. The cookies are easy and quick to make and their name literally means "Hurry, guests are coming!"

2 eggs
1 cup granulated sugar
1 cup honey
1 teaspoon vanilla
2 teaspoons baking soda
1 tablespoon water
4 1/2 cups all-purpose flour
2 teaspoons baking powder
1 teaspoon salt
1 egg, beaten, for glaze
Sugar for sprinkling

1. Preheat oven to 350°.
2. In a large bowl, beat eggs until light and fluffy. Add sugar, honey and vanilla and whisk until blended.
3. In a small bowl, dissolve the baking soda in water and add to the egg/honey mixture.
4. Sift flour, baking powder and salt together and gradually add into the egg/honey mixture until a soft dough forms.
5. Divide dough in half and on a floured surface, roll half the dough to 1/8-inch thickness. Cut into shapes with cookie cutters. Place on baking sheet and brush tops with beaten egg. Sprinkle with sugar and bake for approximately 12 minutes. Repeat with remaining dough.

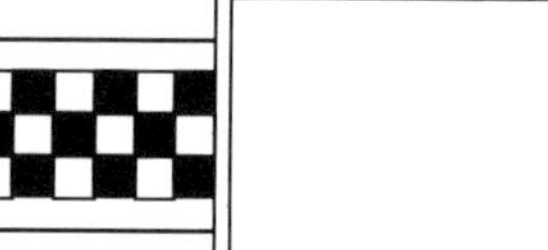

Brown Rice Pudding

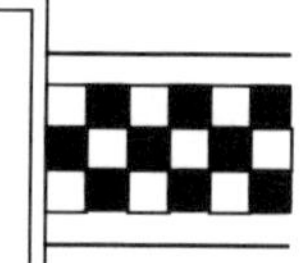

From Walbrook **Serves 6**

This is an interesting version of rice pudding. It is not as creamy as traditional rice pudding, but the addition of egg whites gives it a very light texture.

3 1/4 cups non-fat powdered milk
1 1/4 cups skim milk
1 ripe banana
4 egg whites, beaten until foamy
1 1/2 cups frozen concentrated apple juice (undiluted)
2 teaspoons vanilla
1 cup cooked long-grain brown rice
2/3 cup raisins, plumped in hot water for 15 minutes

TOPPING
1 teaspoon ground cinnamon
1 teaspoon ground nutmeg
1 cup grape nuts

1. Preheat oven to 350°.
2. In a saucepan, combine powdered and skim milk and bring to a simmer. Remove from heat and reserve.
3. In a food processor or blender, purée banana, add beaten egg whites, apple concentrate and vanilla and blend well. Pour into cooled milk.
4. In a 1-quart casserole, add cooked rice and raisins. Pour in milk mixture and bake for 35 minutes.
5. Meanwhile make topping by mixing together all ingredients.
6. Remove from oven, sprinkle with topping mixture and continue cooking another 25–35 minutes. Serve warm or cold.

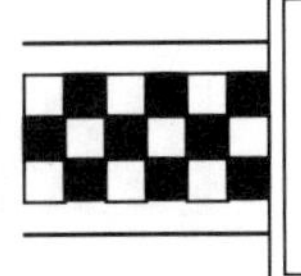

Pudim Fla a Fernanda (Flan Pudding)

From Highlandtown **Portuguese** ***Serves 6***

A wonderful dessert that can be made a day ahead. Bring to room temperature before serving.

CARAMEL
1/2 cup granulated sugar
1/4 cup water

CUSTARD
6 eggs
6 tablespoons granulated sugar
1/2 teaspoon vanilla
2 1/2 cups milk

1. To make caramel, heat sugar and water together in a heavy saucepan over medium heat, stirring constantly until sugar has turned a medium brown color. Do not cook to dark brown or caramel will taste bitter.
2. In a 12-inch tube pan or in 6 1-cup ramekins, spread the caramel mixture evenly on the bottom, working quickly as caramel hardens almost immediately.
3. Preheat oven to 350°.
4. To make custard, beat eggs in a bowl until light and fluffy. Add sugar and vanilla and beat again.
5. In a saucepan, gently warm milk until tepid. Slowly pour into the egg mixture, whisking constantly.
6. Strain the mixture into another bowl. (This will remove any sediments and will make a smoother custard.) Pour this over the caramel and bake for 1 hour. Cool and refrigerate.
7. To serve, slide a knife around the rim of tube pan or ramekins and turn out onto a serving plate.

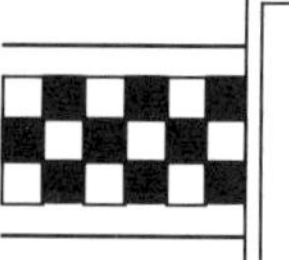

Boiled Apple Dumplings

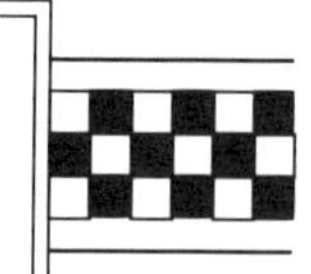

From Mt. Vernon ***Makes 8 dumplings***

An unusual but delicious dessert. Be sure to cook the dumplings for at least 20 minutes. They are best served at once with the custard.

1 apple, peeled, cut in half, cored, then each half quartered (8 pieces)
1/2 teaspoon ground nutmeg
1/2 teaspoon ground cinnamon
1/2 teaspoon granulated sugar

BISCUIT DOUGH
2 cups all-purpose flour
2 teaspoons baking powder
1/2 teaspoon salt
1 tablespoon vegetable shortening
About 3/4 cup milk

CUSTARD SAUCE
2 tablespoons corn flour
2 tablespoons granulated sugar
2 cups milk
3 eggs

1. In a bowl, place apples, nutmeg, cinnamon and sugar and toss together.
2. To make biscuit dough, in a bowl, add flour, baking powder and salt. Cut in shortening, then gradually add in enough milk to form a soft dough. Cut dough in half.
3. On a floured surface, roll out 1 portion of dough to approximately 1/8-inch thickness. Cut into quarters and trim into approximately 3–4-inch squares. Place 1 piece of apple in center of each square and wrap dough around apple piece, enclosing it completely.

Pinch edges to seal. (A little water may be used to seal dough firmly.) Repeat with remaining apple pieces and dough.

4. Bring a large saucepan of water to a boil. Gently lower the dumplings into the water. Cover and boil dumplings for approximately 20 minutes. Remove with a slotted spoon and place on a platter. Reserve.
5. To make custard, in a saucepan, mix corn flour and sugar together and add a little milk to form a paste. Heat the rest of the milk until tepid and pour into corn flour mixture. Place over a double boiler and stir continuously until mixture thickens. Remove from heat and cool. Beat in eggs, one at a time, until well incorporated. Continue cooking at a simmer for about 8–10 minutes, or until slightly thickened.
6. Place dumplings in a bowl and pour custard on top. Serve warm.

Variation: For baked apple dumplings, place wrapped apples seam side down in a buttered casserole. In a small saucepan, heat together 3 tablespoons maple syrup, 3 tablespoons water and 2 tablespoons butter. Pour over dumplings and bake in a 350° oven for 10–15 minutes. Serve with custard sauce.

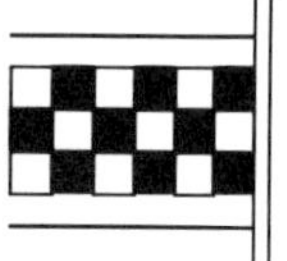

Tart Crust

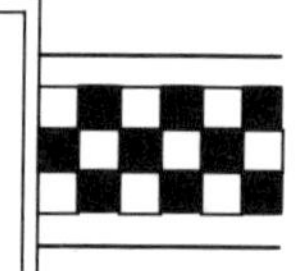

From Inner Harbor ***Makes 1 9-inch crust***

We offer a few tips to help in baking a pastry crust blind successfully. When placing rolled-out dough into a pie dish make sure you press the dough firmly against sides of bottom of dish. Prick bottom of crust and place in freezer for 20–30 minutes before baking.

1 1/4 cups all-purpose flour
Pinch of salt
6 tablespoons cold unsalted butter, cut into pieces
2 tablespoons cold vegetable shortening
3–4 tablespoons ice water

1. If making by hand, combine flour and salt in a bowl. Cut in butter and shortening until mixture resembles coarse meal. Add ice water a tablespoon at a time, sprinkling it over the flour and tossing it with a fork until it comes together to form a dough. Form dough into a ball, flatten it slightly, cover with plastic wrap and chill 30 minutes. Remove from refrigerator, place on a floured surface and roll into a 12-inch round. Fit into a 9-inch tart pan with a removable bottom and crimp the excess dough from the fluted edges. Prick the bottom of the shell with a fork, cover and chill for 30 minutes before baking. Bake in a 350° oven for about 25 minutes, or until lightly golden.
2. If making with a food processor, combine flour and salt in the bowl of a processor fitted with a steel blade. Add butter and shortening and whiz several times until mixture resembles coarse meal. Pour ice water a drop at a time through the feed tube with the machine running until dough forms into a ball. Remove dough ball, flatten slightly, cover with plastic wrap and chill for 30 minutes. Roll out and bake as described above.

Index

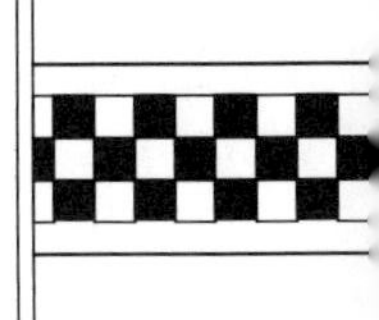